IN MY HEAD

To Kimberly -
Best wishes to you!
God Bless !

Melody Cope

IN MY HEAD

Living My Life with Bi-Polar

Melody Hope

To order additional copies of this book, contact:
Xlibris Corporation
1-888-795-4274
www.Xlibris.com
Orders@Xlibris.com
40622

CONTENTS

Acknowledgement

For my Daddy: I hold dear in my heart the memories of all the times we shared together. I love you, Daddy.

To my Mother: I admire you for the person you are. I do not know how to express in words what you mean to me. I love you so very, very much.

To my sisters, Debbie and Teresa: Thank you for your unconditional love, and never giving up hope on me. Without you I don't know if I would be dead or alive. I love you both more than you will ever know.

To my children, Tara, Kayla, and Trey: I love you to the sky and back. You are my jewels I will treasure forever.

To my husband, Tommy: Thank you for all you do for me. I love you with all my heart.

To my wonderful friend, Tracy: Thank you for your caring words, your sense of humor, and for letting me know I can count on you always. I love you.

To my psychiatrist, Dr. Joseph P. Arisco: It was you that helped me realize the seriousness of having bi-polar disorder, and the need to be responsible to follow through with my treatment. Thank you.

To Briana Sutton: Thank you for the excellent job you did on the cover art.

To Terry Spearman: Thank you for doing the copy-editing on my book.

As A Child

My mother raised me in church. I was taught that God so loved me that he gave his only begotten Son that I might have eternal life. Learning more and more about God, I came to have faith and hope, and found comfort in knowing God loved me.

My mother was a wonderful person with a sweet spirit. She was a caring and giving person, and I looked up to her and admired her. She was perfect in every way to me, and I wanted to be perfect just as she was.

My mother and father divorced when I was around six years old. I don't think I had started school yet when he left. I rarely saw him, and I didn't ask where he was; nor was I told.

I was born in Tyler, Texas and I lived in Kirk Patrick Addition off of Hwy 64. I lived in that addition all through elementary and junior high school. There were six streets in our neighborhood, and through the years we lived on four of the six streets.

As a child, I played outside all the time, walking and running up and down the streets with the other kids in my neighborhood. I played dolls with the two girls down the street in their front yard. I climbed trees and played hopscotch and tag. I loved to be outside playing. I went outside in the morning and stayed outside until dark. I didn't play inside; for me there was nothing to do inside.

My grandmother, Nonnie, lived on the last street in our neighborhood. We usually went to her house on Sunday's after church to eat dinner. She was a great cook who made everything from scratch. Almost every time I went to her house, she was cooking or sewing. When I walked through the door, I could smell the aroma of her cooking. When she made homemade rolls, I watched her make the dough and then knead it as I stood beside her in her kitchen. She would roll it out on her counter top, and pinched off small pieces and rolled them in little balls. She placed three small balls in each section of her muffin pan. Once she took them out of the oven, I would get one out of the pan and spread lots of butter all inside of the roll. I would eat it hot right out of the oven, and it melted in my mouth. Everything she cooked was so tasty. Nonnie worked at a sewing factory for several years, and sewed most all the clothes she wore. There were several spools of thread in her sewing room, and a few thimbles. My cousins and I played a game we called, hide-the-thimble, when we were at her house, and we had lots of fun.

When I was in the first grade we lived on Coleman Street. At night I began to cry and scream loudly, and complained of having a stomachache. This went on for awhile, so Mother decided to have me admitted in the hospital. My first grade teacher from school, Mrs. Odem, sent flowers to me from her, and my classmates. I felt special, and thought they must truly like me.

I stayed in the hospital for a night or two, and there were several tests the doctor had done to find out what was wrong with me. I was released from the hospital, and they did not find anything that was causing any pain, or why I screamed, and cried. My daddy had left home shortly before we moved to the house on Coleman Street. Was I missing him, and crying for him?

One of the houses we lived in had an attic fan. On spring nights the windows were raised, and the attic fan blew in a pleasant breeze on my face. I liked lying in my bed with the curtains slightly blowing, and smelling the freshness of outside. On those nights I would sleep like a baby.

Another house we lived in was on Sycamore Street, which was a house my aunt and uncle owned. It was wood framed, and the color of the house was painted a light pink. Through the front door, there was a small entryway, then to left there were three steps that led to a sunk-in living room. At the other end of the living room were three more steps, which led to a big open area where the dining room and kitchen was. It had a long hallway, three bedrooms, and one bathroom. A carport was attached to the house, and a tall oak tree was growing against one side of it. I would climb up the tree and step onto the roof of the carport. Then I would make my way to the rooftop of the house. I always went to the back part of the roof, and there I would sit day dreaming, and looking up at the sky. It was my own private place where I would go often.

I met a girl named Bonnie while living on Sycamore Street. She lived on the other side of the street, three houses down, in a white wood framed house. She was my first best friend. She was also the first girl I knew that didn't have a daddy at home. I never saw her daddy, so I assumed she lived with just her mom like I did. She was skinny like I was, and had long stringy brown hair, just like me. She was maybe a year younger than I was. She had really big, pretty brown eyes. They seemed to twinkle when she talked. I felt like Bonnie and I had a lot in common, and I loved playing with her, which we did almost every day.

I collected Coke bottles around the neighborhood, gathering them in my arms and walking to the store once I had four or five. The store was five to six blocks down the road and across Hwy 64. I was barefoot a lot while I was playing outside. I did walk down the road, but mostly I skipped and hopped. Often I walked to the store barefoot. Though the road would be unbearably hot, that didn't matter to me. I kept right on walking, skipping, and hopping all the way to the store. When my feet couldn't take the hot road, I hopped on the grass, dodging the sticker burrs until my feet could stand the hot road again.

When I arrived at the store, I gave my Coke bottles to the lady who worked there. Each bottle was worth five cents. I stayed at the store for awhile looking at all the boxes of candy. My favorite was the banana bites, tootsie rolls, the little wax bottles filled with juice, and gum. I would buy a little brown paper sack full of penny candy and then walked, skipped, and hopped back home with my little sack. I was so excited to get my bag of candy, even though it took only a few minutes to eat it.

I was taught to always put others before myself. Mother had a birthday party for me in our front yard on Sycamore Street when I turned nine. Six or seven of my friends came to my party, and Bonnie was there. She gave me a small stuffed dog that had bright red fuzzy hair, and long ears. It's tail, which was covered with long hair, just as it's ears did, came with a brush and comb. I loved it, especially since Bonnie gave it to me. It was a perfect, beautiful day. The grass was green, there was a slight breeze, and the sun was shining bright. Mother set a card table up with the birthday cake, red punch, forks and napkins on it.

When it came time to cut the cake, we formed a line, and Mother gave each one of my friends a piece of cake, and a cup of punch. I was the last one she gave some to, and I didn't know why, after all, it was my birthday party.

We ran around the yard laughing, and playing. We formed a line again to play pin-the-tail-on-the-donkey. Mother had me get at the back of the line, and be the last one, just as she did when she served the cake and punch. I was the one that was to go first because it was my birthday. Why did my friends get to go first? It didn't seem fair, but I assumed it was because I was always to put others before myself. What Mother did was always the right thing, even if I didn't understand. I wondered why I was to put others before myself, even at my birthday party.

Not long, maybe a few months after my birthday, Bonnie moved. She was gone now, and I knew I would miss her tremendously.

Mother and I went to church all the time. We were members of West Erwin Baptist Church, and we went every Sunday morning, Sunday evening, Wednesday evening, for Thursday visitation night, choir practice, and any other function at church. West Erwin Baptist Church was an old building. It was wood framed and sat on top of a hill. There were several red steps to climb that led to the church door. The wood floor would creak as you walked across it. Mother had taken me to church from the time I was a baby.

When I was maybe five or six years old, a brand new church was built just a few blocks down the road from our church. The old church was left empty, and the new church is where we now went. Then, it wasn't long, and another part was built on to the church. It was beautiful inside, and it had a balcony that was so high up. I didn't go up the stairs to the balcony very often. The carpet was blue and the pews were covered with blue velvet. There were huge chandeliers hanging from the tall ceiling, and the light bulbs were shaped like little candles.

While Mother had choir practice, I ran and played all through the church with my friends, even though, I wasn't to run in church. I loved going to church. Everybody there were like my family, and I found love and comfort there.

I was always with Mother at church, but it didn't seem that Mother was at home with me much. Mother was always at work, but if she was at home, she would usually be in her bedroom reading her bible.

Mother smiled and laughed as she talked to the people at church. She sang in the choir and taught a Sunday school class. The church had a bus ministry with three or four buses, and she was a part of that ministry, too, with her own bus that took little children to church. Once, a man came to our church and taught a sign language class. Of course, my mother learned sign language and started a deaf ministry. She met deaf people and invited them to church. She told them about God through her hands as she interpreted for the preacher. She was beautiful standing in front of the church with her hands, her arms, and her body flowing so easily and making sure the deaf people could learn about God and the church. The deaf people would sing in their language and smile in joyfulness. My mother also taught a class at church so that other people could communicate with the deaf. Tears would sometimes fill my eyes when I was old enough to see and understand what she was doing for these people. She took the talent God gave her to reach out to them. She helped the deaf people know and feel the Holy Spirit.

When we left church, Mother's smiles, her laughter, her excitement, her joyfulness, and her caring spirit were left behind at church. It was as though I was looking out a window reaching for all the things she did for people and the attention she gave to people. I yearned to have that part of her.

Mother didn't give me hugs or kisses. She didn't tuck me in bed at night or play with me when I was young girl. As a child, I never heard her say to me, "I love you."

It seemed as though I never had her for myself. In my heart, I always told myself, "Mother does love me." I knew she did, but I had mixed feelings about what love was. I loved church, and church was where I saw love as I watched all the other children get hugs and kisses from their mothers. I would hear their mothers tell their boys and girls "I love you."

How could I ever be perfect like my mother? I wanted my mother to see me like she saw other people. I wanted to hear her words, and have affection of love from her.

We never had any "girl talks." She never told me about the world outside of church. I had to learn about the bad parts of life on my own as I grew older. I had to learn I was not perfect like Mother. Growing up, I just wanted to please my mother and be as good as she was. I wanted Mother to tell me she was proud of me. I wanted to hear her tell me I was pretty. I wanted to know why Mother didn't tell me these things.

I never stopped trying to please Mother. I always wanted happiness for her, and I wanted her to be happy all the time like she was at church. But I never could make Mother happy; someone else had to do that.

I didn't know my daddy very well and I wasn't around him much at all. I didn't know how it would be to have a daddy at home. As a child, I never felt angry or deprived because Daddy wasn't around, because he wasn't a part of my life. I seldom wondered where Daddy was. I didn't know what I was missing from Daddy's not being there with us. I didn't think of how to make Daddy be there, I didn't know how it would make a difference in my life seeing him more often. I just knew I had a daddy, and that's what mattered to me.

I have two sisters. Debbie is the oldest, and she's seven years older than I. My other sister, Teresa, is five years older. I don't remember Debbie or Teresa being at home very much.

Debbie is the sister in whom, as a child, I found innocence and kindness. She was prim and proper, and she was quiet with a soft, sweet voice. She was beautiful, but it never seemed to me that she was aware of her beauty. Her smooth skin and her perfect brown hair was like that of a beauty queen.

Teresa was the adventurous one. She was full of life, she laughed a lot, and she was out to have fun. She had lots of friends, probably because of her boundless enthusiasm. She also was beautiful. She made her make-up so perfect when she applied it. She wore hip puggers and body shirts, with her belt around her small hips. She dressed as perfectly as she made up her face. She had long brown hair that also always looked perfect. Teresa was going to do exactly what she wanted to do. She was the outgoing one who didn't seem to have to be anything but who she was. It didn't seem to matter to her what anybody else thought.

I was the one that couldn't find exactly how to show my personality. I wanted Debbie's sweetness and her beauty. I also wanted the bubbly and fearless part of Teresa.

But I was shy. I definitely didn't want to draw any attention to myself. I was quite like Debbie. I didn't want to be quiet all the time, though. Why couldn't I open up and say what I wanted to say? Why couldn't I say what I felt inside? I hadn't yet mastered the part of Teresa I wanted to be like. I didn't want to be afraid to say or do what I wanted. I didn't want to be afraid that what I said would come out wrong. I didn't want to be afraid that I wouldn't do anything right. Teresa never seemed to be afraid to say or do what she wanted to do.

As a young child, I played and had fun. I didn't have the fear of being embarrassed around the other kids I played with then. I didn't think about saying or doing something wrong. I had fun and felt happy. I was very self-conscious when I began junior high school. I enjoyed going to school and being with my friends. They were cheerleaders, but I couldn't be a cheerleader; I wouldn't be a good one. I couldn't be in the band because I was sure I wouldn't be able to learn how to plan an instrument. I just knew I couldn't be good at those things, so I wouldn't even try. It was hard for me to look at someone in the eyes. I felt they would find flaws in me. I thought they would think I was ugly. I was afraid when I talked to someone that I would say the wrong thing or that they would laugh at me. I felt I would be a failure at almost anything I tried to do, so I didn't give myself a chance to fail. I kept quiet around most everyone except for my few close friends.

Mother never asked how my day was at school. She never asked if I had homework or what kind of grades I was making. I didn't get encouragement to make good grades in school. I didn't really get any encouragement from her; I didn't expect it from her.

One thing I did love was going to church and singing in the church choir. I sang in the children's choir, in the pre-teen choir, and in the young adult choir, as I grew older. I did enjoy singing, and I felt somewhat confident that I sang pretty well, in part because the lady who taught the songs to us had a way of making me feel I did sing well. I loved all the singing in the church, and it gave me a joyful feeling inside. I loved all the people I knew at church, and I had great friends there.

When I was thirteen years old a new street was added to our neighborhood, and we moved into a brand-new house on that street, Rosecrest Lane. It was the first brand-new home we ever had. It was prettier than any of the other houses we had lived in, and I was happy that we were moving into our own home.

Mother's favorite color was orange. In our living room, we had an orange vinyl couch. The carpet was shag with orange in it. We had a Curtis Mathis TV. We also had a dark green recliner in there.

The kitchen was rather small. We had one telephone, and it hung on the wall in the kitchen, and it had a long cord that reached almost into the living room. We had our kitchen table in the dining room, but we didn't ever sit as a family at the table to eat supper. There was one time, though, Mother, Debbie, Teresa and I did sit and eat at the table. Even Daddy was there. It was a special evening to sit down, and eat supper all together.

Daddy came to our house on Rosecrest Lane sometimes. I saw him more now, than I had any other time in my life. He was there the night we ate supper at the dinner table, and he was at home at Christmas that year. He came to our house a few times, and waited at the door for Mother, and they would leave together. I stayed home, and I didn't know where they went. He didn't say much, he was very quite when he was at the house. Daddy and Mother had remarried, but I wasn't told they had. I never noticed him staying overnight. Then it wasn't long before he wasn't there at all. Come to find out, they had separated.

Mother had let Debbie and Teresa decide how they wanted their bedrooms decorated. Debbie had red, white, and blue shag carpet in her bedroom and a huge United States flag hanging on her wall. She had a full-size bed and a big, nice dresser.

Teresa picked pink and purple shag carpet for our bedroom, which I shared with her. We had twin beds with purple-bed spreads. She had a record player that sat on a table in between the two beds.

Our bathroom was big. Sometimes I would stand at the door to the bathroom and watch Teresa put on her make-up. She would primp as she made her face look perfect. Teresa always seemed excited to start her day, and she had to be one of the prettiest girls in school as well as a terrific personality. Debbie didn't ever seem to be at home.

Mother had a big bedroom outfitted with a fancy bedroom suit, and she had her sewing machine in her bedroom. She had a bathroom all to herself. I would go in her bathroom sometimes and look through all the costume jewelry she had in a big, pretty jewelry box. Mother wore necklaces and earrings that matched, and she always had her nails polished. She was an attractive lady.

Neither Debbie nor Teresa was ever at home in the evenings. They were always gone, so I didn't talk much to either of them. There didn't ever seem to be any time that we were together. Our home had very little conversation in it. Debbie got married when she was seventeen years old, and then she was gone. Teresa got married when she was barely sixteen; then she was gone, too. They lived in our new home very briefly.

Now it was just Mother and me. It didn't seem much different, since I hadn't been around Debbie and Teresa much anyway. The house seemed empty, though. The bedrooms were no longer my sisters' own private place to go if they needed to be alone. The red, white and blue were left behind. The pink and purple was also left behind.

I chose Debbie's bedroom to be mine now, and mother bought me an even fancier bedroom suit than hers' for my room. I had a bedroom all to myself now. I believed I would live in our new home until I got married.

I stayed alone in my bedroom a lot. This was the time in my life when I found comfort in writing. I would get paper and a pen and write while I sat on my bed. I would write all the feelings I had on paper. I wrote most often when I was sad. When I got upset or angry about something that had happened, I would write everything I was feeling, and it made me feel better for some reason. I truly enjoyed writing. It wasn't just the fact of pouring my feelings out on paper; I also enjoyed trying to make my handwriting look pretty. I wrote in all different ways. I would print or write cursive. I would write big and small. I didn't care how my writing looked when I was mad. My handwriting seemed to match my feelings. When I finished writing what was on my mind, I sometimes kept it. At times, I would wad it up really fast and tight; then I would throw it in the trash. If I wrote when I was mad or felt hurt, I would tear the paper in tiny pieces when I finished writing about what had happened. I would let them fall from my hands into the trash. Sometimes I would let them fall from my hands onto the floor. One piece would fall, then several pieces, until the last piece left my hands. Then I would pick up all the pieces and throw them in the trash.

I didn't ever talk to anyone about how I was feeling. I was very private and my feelings were very personal to me. Why should I tell anyone? Pen and paper is the way I expressed my feelings. I could write anything I wanted without holding any of the feelings back. I felt much better after I finished writing what was inside of me that I couldn't share.

The fear of not being good enough at what I wanted to try to do came in my early teens. Being insecure about myself began when I entered junior high school. As a child, it seemed natural to be who I was. The hard part was growing older and having to find out who I was.

I was alone at home much of the time. If Mother was there, we weren't talking or watching TV together, or anything else. We did our own things. My thing was being in my bedroom. I would talk to my friends on the phone, or I would write, or sleep. I slept a lot.

I went to the movies with my friends sometimes on the weekend. There was a couple across the street from us who had five children, and sometimes I would watch their children for them when they went out on Saturday nights. I enjoyed babysitting them and playing with them. I felt important taking care of them, and I had fun with them. They were a perfect family.

In the eighth grade, I began to go to parties my friends had. I had my first boy/girl party at my sister, Teresa's house. We played spin-the-bottle, which was the first time I had played that game. We went outside, and we would talk amongst each other. The boys stayed a few hours then left, and the girls stayed overnight. I had my first beer at my party, and I had also started smoking cigarettes at that time in my life, not in an effort to fit in; I actually enjoyed smoking.

One friend of mine had a party at her house, and that was where I had my first sexual experience. A boy took me into the bathroom. There was kissing, and then we got in the bathtub, the clothes went off and he was lying on top of me. I was so scared; I didn't know what to do. He was trying to have his way with me, and I kept telling him to stop. I was getting mad, so I slapped him hard, and he got up. I felt horrible, completely horrible. I was so ashamed. It all happened so fast. The next day, I went to school, and heard that the story was that I had "put out." I was so afraid I was pregnant, but of course, I couldn't be pregnant, he had not even entered me. I was so naive about it all. I truly despised that boy and hated the thought of ever having sex.

When I was fourteen years old, the teenagers at my church were going to Snow Camp. I had gone the year before, and I was going to go this time, too. I would get to miss school for a week since we were going during the winter. We were going in the church bus to Colorado and stay a full week there. I made a list of things to pack. I wrote down how many pairs of socks, how many pairs of underwear, my toothbrush, my toothpaste, my hairbrush, what clothes I would wear, every single thing I thought I would need. I packed it all in my suitcase, and Mother took me to church the next morning. That day I saw the Moms giving their kids hugs and kisses, and they were telling their kids they loved them and to have a good time. My mother simply told me goodbye. I didn't understand why my mother didn't give me a hug or a kiss, or even tell me she loved me. When I saw how much affection the other Moms gave their kids, I realized how much I wanted all of that from my mother, and I felt really sad. When we all got on the bus to go, my sadness went away rather quickly, because I was ready for Snow Camp. I was going to have a great time.

We went to church services every evening at Snow Camp. One night during the church services, I was listening very closely to what the preacher was saying. It was as if he were speaking to only me. I was getting a strange feeling. The preacher was telling us how we could be saved. He told us all we needed to do was to ask Jesus to forgive us of our sins, and ask him to come into our hearts. I thought back and realized something: I didn't ever remember praying and asking God to save me after all this time of going to church. Now, while listening to the preacher, I felt I wasn't because I could not remember praying that prayer. I wanted to know for sure that Jesus was truly in my heart. I wanted to know without a shadow of a doubt that I would go to heaven to be with God.

As I sat there in my thoughts, I was very touched. My heart was beating fast. Should I walk down the aisle in front of all these people and my friends? It didn't matter though who else was there; this is what I needed and wanted to do. I took that first step and walked down the aisle. The preacher's wife from my church knelt down beside me. She began to read from her Bible, John 3:16. I cried, and I prayed for God to forgive my sins and asked Jesus to come into my heart. The feeling I had when I finished praying was peace and comfort and happiness. I knew now I was born again. I was so excited to be a child of God's, and everyone else shared my excitement. The feeling I had, I wanted to keep forever. I would never forget this night. I didn't have to wonder if I had really been saved anymore. I knew I was. I knew I was going to heaven, and I knew God would always be with me. I had known for a long time God was always with me, but now I felt it in my heart.

I had a great time at Snow Camp. On the bus going back home, I was carrying that feeling I had when I knelt and prayed my prayer for salvation. I couldn't believe the joy I had in my heart. I saw my mother waiting for me when the bus pulled in the church parking lot, and I couldn't wait to tell her what happened. She would be so excited. As Mother was pulling out of the church parking lot, I told her I had been saved. She simply said, "That's good."

I didn't get the hug from Mother that I was sure I would get. Why wasn't she glad? Why wasn't she as excited as I was? She was always telling people about God and how they could be saved. I didn't know why Mother wasn't telling me she was happy for me. My new-found love from God made me happy, and nothing would ever change that.

Our church started a private school at the beginning of my ninth grade, but I went to the public school I had gone to all through junior high. After I got back from Snow Camp, I told Mother I wanted to go to our church school. I thought it would be the right thing to do, and I wanted to do all that I should now that I was saved. I left my friends behind at my public school and joined the friends I had at my church.

Mother bought the uniforms everyone wore at the church school: navy blue skirts with blue jackets and white shirts. We also had red suits just the same as the blue ones. I thought Mother would be happy that I decided to go to our church school, but if she was happy about it, I didn't see it.

I wasn't making good grades at my public school, but Mother didn't ask me about my grades. She just signed my report cards and never made any comments. When I started going to the church school, my grades didn't improve. At that time, grades didn't seem to matter to me. I just wanted to have fun. I missed my friends, but the ones I went to school with now were good friends, too. I had known most of them for a long time.

I would think back of Daddy at times. When I was around Daddy, I felt happy. I saw Daddy smile, and I felt that he was happy, too. He once took a friend of mine and me to the movies. He sang the song on the radio, "Like a Rhinestone Cowboy." While he sang the song, I smiled as I sat beside him in his truck. I sat beside him in church one Sunday morning. I was around twelve years old. We stood up to sing a church hymnal. Daddy sang the song as I looked at him with pride. The times I had with my daddy were few and far between, so they were very special to me. I loved Daddy, and I loved every time I saw him.

On Daddy's birthday, when he turned forty-two, I bought him a present. I was thirteen years old. Mother knew how to reach him. I called him on the phone, and I asked him to come to the house. I told him I had bought him a present, which was a bottle of Old English Leather cologne, the only cologne I knew that Daddy wore. When Daddy came to the house and knocked on the door, I opened the door, but he didn't come in. I went outside in our garage with him and handed him his present. I hugged him and told him, "I love you" for the first and last time.

It wasn't long after Daddy had his forty-second birthday that Mother got a phone call in the middle of the night. My aunt came over, and Mother told me she had to go to the hospital to check on Daddy. I didn't know why he was at the hospital. Mother left with my aunt. The thought came to mind, as I was alone at my house: Daddy's gone. It was as if someone told me, "Daddy's dead." When my mother came home with my aunt, she put her arms around me for the first time that I knew of. As she had her arms around me, she said, "He's gone." I knew what she meant; he had passed away. My mother was broken; she seemed to fight back the tears that were in her eyes. I didn't know how I should feel. It was strange to see my mother broken-hearted. I knew she loved Daddy now. She put the pieces back together. Mother's weakness turned quickly back to her strength, as it always had. It seemed right away that people were coming to our house bringing food and their condolences to Mother. I didn't want to be around the people. I just wanted to be alone. I went outside, took my ball, threw it on the top of the roof of our house, and watched it roll down over and over. A couple of my friends called me that night, but I told them I couldn't talk; my Daddy had died. I will never forget that night seeing Mother broken-hearted.

I knew Daddy was a good man; I knew it in my heart. It didn't matter to me he didn't come to see me often. It didn't matter to me where he was when I was a child. I was proud he was my daddy, and I was thankful for all the times I had been with him.

When Mother said to me, "He's gone." I knew he had gone home to be with God in Heaven. His tombstone was appropriately chiseled out, "Gone Home."

After a year had past since Daddy had died, Mother had not gone out with any men. Church and work was her life, and always had been. She did go out with her friends from church sometimes, with whom she laughed, and I could see she enjoyed being with them.

I was lonely; I was alone so much of the time at home. I spent most of my time in my room with my thoughts all to myself. So many times when I got home from school I would fix a big plate of french fries, sit down, and eat them.

I would also eat frito chips with french onion dip. Mother did always make sure we had my favorite chips and dip.

I would sleep almost every day when I got home from school after I ate something. Mother and I still didn't sit at the table to eat supper. I found something to eat and I don't know what she ate.

A man came to our house one evening to visit with Mother, and immediately, I couldn't stand him, even though I didn't know him. I was very rude to him. This was the first man that had come to our house to visit with Mother since Daddy had died. Mother didn't say anything to me about being rude to him after he left. I didn't see him again after that night. I don't know why; maybe Mother didn't like him, either.

Mother rarely ever punished me. I had never gotten a spanking from her. I respected her, and I wanted to do all that she expected me to do. Of course, when I was a teenager, there were times she would get aggravated with me. Usually, it was when I kept on asking her why I couldn't do something I wanted to do, after she had told me no.

There was one time, a friend was spending the night with me and we went to the movies with another friend, Sally, from school. Her mother took us to the movies, but we didn't know who was going to bring us home. Sally's mother was taking us, but she was not going to bring us back to my house, but Mother thought she was. We went to the movies anyway thinking we would be able to find someone to take us back to my house. When it was time to go home, we asked a couple of boys that we knew that were older than us to take us to my house. Mother was always in bed when I would get back home from going to the movies. I knew she would not know we had gotten those boys to bring us back from the movies. My friend and I were in the kitchen, and the phone rang. I picked up the phone and it was Mother. Where was she? I was sure she was in bed. She was at my grandmothers' house just a couple of blocks from where we lived.

Mother asked, "How did you get home?"

I didn't know what to say, but before I could say anything, Mother said, "You are grounded!" I could hear in her voice that she was very angry with me.

"I called Sally's mother, and she told me she had not brought you home." Mother said.

Mother came home and she said to me, "I will talk to you tomorrow about this."

The next morning my friend went home and I was sure Mother was going to tell me I was grounded. But, she never said another word to me about it. I felt horrible because I had lied to my mother, and that was something I knew I should never do.

I was fifteen years old when Mother's best friend from childhood, whom she went to school with, introduced her to a man. He lived in the same town Mother's friend lived, right where she and Mother had gone to school together. Mother dated this man for close to a year, and then they were married.

I was very upset and sad when I found out we would be moving to another town, but I wouldn't let Mother know I was upset about it. This is what Mother wanted. I dealt with my feelings by locking them up inside of me. I wanted to do anything to have my mother be happy. I didn't ask any questions about moving; it just happened.

I was leaving the neighborhood I had grown up in. I was going to be leaving my friends that I had had for a long time. The friends that I could laugh with, spend time with, and have fun with. They had become my escape from the loneliness I felt at home. I told myself I would be all right; I had to be. I had gone to the same church since I was a baby, and I would miss the people there whom I had known for several years.

I didn't like the town where we moved. I had to find new friends, something I wasn't good at. It was a small town, with a population of about five hundred. It seemed everyone was born and raised there, or they had been there for most of their lives. I just didn't feel like I would ever fit in. I missed all my friends I had left behind.

After we moved I continued going to the church school for the remaining of my ninth grade. Mother allowed me to miss one day of school and go to the school I would attend at the beginning of my sophomore year with my mother's best friend's daughter. I saw a boy there that day, walking down the hall without a shirt on, and I couldn't believe that he was allowed to do that. He had sandy blonde hair and a beautiful smile. He was the cutest boy I had ever seen.

Throughout my life I had learned to be responsible. My Mother received social security checks after Daddy died, and when she married she gave me the checks. I opened a checking account and deposited my checks every month in my bank account. I got a summer job at a grocery store after my sophomore year. I liked the job all right and I did like making extra money. As a cashier there, having to hand key all the prices in on the register, I was always afraid I would ring up the wrong price.

I bought my own clothes and whatever else I needed. I bought a car when I was fifteen, a rally sport Camero. I paid the monthly payments for my car, and I did learn how to manage money, which was a good thing.

I wanted Mother and I to have a closer relationship than we did when I was younger. She meant everything to me. I saw how many peoples' lives that she touched. I know she was a good friend to so many, and I could tell that others looked up to her, too. As a child, I had hoped to grow up to be a person like her. What I really always wanted from Mother was her attention and affection. Mother did show me that I would always have guidance, strength, and the ultimate love from God. In spite of everything, I always held on to my faith.

Mother and I began going to church where we moved. One Sunday morning, I saw the boy I had seen walking down the hall without a shirt on at school. He was sitting in the pew behind me. We stood up to sing, and my bible was lying on the pew where I was sitting. When I went to sit back down my bible wasn't there. I turned around and looked at the boy, and he had my bible. I smiled at him, then he gave my bible back to me.

The first day of school I saw the boy again. I had found out his name was Kyle. We became boyfriend and girlfriend a few weeks later, and became inseparable. We broke up, but just for a few months, and then we were back together. I liked him a lot. He gave me a promise ring, that school year, he gave me an engagement ring my junior year. We were in love, and I was anxious to get married.

Starting a Family

The summer after my junior year, Kyle graduated, and we married in June. I was seventeen years old, and he was eighteen.

My wedding was beautiful. I wore a formal gown of white peau d'soie overlayed with silk organza, fashioned in an empire silhouette with v-neckline and long sheer bishop sleeves trimmed in embossed wedding lace. I also wore a triple-tiered, fingertip length veil bordered in lace. Mother made my wedding dress, and she made sure it was just the way I wanted it, exactly like you would see in a brides' magazine. My wedding bouquet was made of white daisies. Mother decorated the church with lovely white and yellow flowers, and candles on a candle obera, and a unity candle. I loved it. I had three bridesmaids, all of them were friends I had gone to school with in junior high. They wore beautiful yellow dresses. Their bouquets were made of yellow daisies. My nieces, Kelly and Caire, were the flower girls, and they wore beautiful yellow dresses also, which Mother had made. I married at West Erwin Baptist, even though I wasn't a member there anymore. Mother was happy on my wedding day, and she hugged me on that day. She also told me I was pretty, words I had been longing to hear from her. She was being affectionate and showing me her love for me for the first time I remember.

I was leaving Mother to begin my life without her, and I was on my way to having a perfect family. I would have a family with a daddy, a momma and our children. I wanted a home full of love with hugs and kisses and the words "I love you" every day. I wanted my family to feel love from me, not just know it.

But, it was hard for me to be affectionate, and I couldn't be affectionate freely. It was something I would have to work at. I always knew my mother loved me, but she didn't show it with hugs and kisses. I wanted desperately to give this affection to my own family.

I didn't have a complete family in my childhood. The husband was missing and the daddy was missing, too. There would be a man in my home now: A husband and a daddy would be a part of my family. What would the role of my husband be? What would my role as a wife be? This had to work. I was determined that my family would be complete. I would have the perfect family.

Kyle was the type who wanted to provide solely for his family. I knew he felt it was the right thing to do, and he made me feel that I didn't need to worry how we would pay the bills. He was kind, hard working, but rather quiet when we were together at home. We didn't ever talk about our plans for the future, but we both knew we wanted to have children.

When it was time for school to start back my senior year, I was ready and determined to graduate. My grades definitely went up in high school. English was my favorite subject; I always liked to write. After all, that's how I was able to express myself as a teenager. Pen to the paper was something I had learned to do. Learning the correct words to use and say was what I wanted to know. I loved bookkeeping and accounting, too, but I was awful at typing. I couldn't type fast enough because I couldn't get past making sure all the words were correctly spelled and there were no mistakes.

In high school, I was still fairly quiet. I began to have a little more self-esteem, and I wasn't as self-conscious, as I had been before. I was feeling like I didn't worry as much if I said something that was wrong. I was finally being able to look at people in the eyes without thinking they were scrutinizing all my flaws. I felt like I was learning that I could be more open and vocal without the fear of rejection.

I went to school faithfully my senior year. I had always gotten myself up and made sure I got on the bus when I was in junior high. Now I was driving myself to school and still getting myself up every morning. I never once thought about staying at home and not going to school. Graduating was something I had to accomplish.

My senior year I had a couple of close friends. I became especially close to two girls in high school, Tracy and Delaine. Having those friends and my determination helped me through my final year of school.

On graduation night, I was truly proud of myself. I was the only one of my family, including my parents, to graduate from high school. I saw that Mother was excited to see my accomplishment. Graduation was by far one of the best days of my life. After all, this made me believe I wasn't a failure. Seeing Mother with a big smile showed me she was proud of me. This was most rewarding for me.

Kyle and I wanted to start our family. Becoming a mother was what I always wanted, and I had always thought of having three or four children. It was finally time to make my dream and goal come true. I was a housewife and that set well with me. I had no idea where I would work or what I would like to do, because the career I wanted was to be the best mother ever.

Kyle made it clear to me that I didn't need to work, unless I wanted to. He went to work at an electric co-op, shortly after we married, and we both were so glad he had gotten the job. We had all we needed, and we did well for ourselves. Kyle worked, and I went to school. When I came home from school, I would fix supper and have it ready when my husband came home from work. We were doing all the right things. Kyle brought home the money and I kept up the house. That was how it was supposed to be.

When we got married, we lived in Kyle's brother's house. After a few months we were able to buy a trailer house, which would be our home, I continued being a housewife. I was bored some days, and some days I would find things to keep me busy. I was happy, and this is what I had always wanted. Marriage suited me well.

Once I went outside on a very windy day to take the trash out. I babysat for my husband's aunt, and I kept her little girl, Dana, for her while she worked. Dana was about four years old, and she was outside with me. I placed a small bag of trash in our burning barrel out in the back of our house. All of a sudden I heard a big boom. I had an aerosol can in the bag of trash, and this is what caused the loud boom. I hadn't thought about it when I threw the match in the barrel. It didn't take but a few seconds, and the flames went rampantly. The flames were rising. They began to go under our trailer house, and I didn't know what to do. I ran inside and got a blanket, went outside with it, and tried to fight the flames back by beating them. The flames had begun to engulf our home. I wanted to try to get some things out of the house. The fire was so hot. The flames got bigger and bigger. I saw that there was nothing I could do to put out the fire.

I began to run through the pasture. It was the hay meadow that my father-in-law cut and bailed hay in. My in-laws lived just right beyond the pasture. I didn't know what to tell Dana to do, and I was so terrified that I just told her to run. I told her to run as fast as she could, "Just run Dana, and don't look back!" As I ran, I made sure Dana was behind me.

I ran yelling as loud as I could, "Fire, fire! Help, help." I was hoping someone would hear my cries. I thought that maybe my in-laws would hear me yelling for help. I was running so fast. Oh, please, let someone come and help me!

My in-laws did hear my cries. To my relief, I saw them driving to me. I wanted someone to put out the blazing fire. They pulled up beside me in their truck, and I climbed in the back. My heart was beating so fast. I couldn't believe our home was burning to the ground. There didn't seem to be anything to do to prevent the fire from engulfing our home.

Now I was yelling, "Get Dana, get Dana!"

She had run as fast as she could. She had to be so scared. I wondered why I didn't carry Dana in my arms, and I felt so guilty for having let her run on her own. What was I thinking? We were safe now, though.

The fire department came out, but it was too late. Our house had burned to the ground. There was nothing left but the tin siding that was all twisted on the ground. Everything in the house had burned completely.

Someone called Kyle at work. He came home and went to his parents' house. I didn't know what I would say to him. I had burned our house down, and this was entirely my fault. What would he say? He would be devastated. How horrible it was going to be for him to see that our home was gone. Everything we had was gone in just a matter of minutes.

When Kyle saw just the ashes of our home, he hugged me. He told me all that mattered was that I was all right. I felt true comfort in his arms.

I couldn't believe this had happened. I was shocked and so very sad. We had things from our wedding shower we had not even unpacked. There were things Kyle had made in school for us, in his agriculture class. He made a beautiful wooden coffee table with a glass top, some wooden lamps, and other things. We had recently gotten a new washer and dryer. The bedroom suit my mother had bought me was gone, as well as my wedding dress. My promise ring, and my graduation ring was also gone. Everything gone. It was all gone. What would we do now?

So many people in the small town we lived in were so giving. They brought lots of clothes for us and gave us money. I will never forget all the people who gave so generously to us.

Kyle and I picked up the pieces and started all over. We would make it through all this. We stayed with Kyle's parents for a brief time, then we moved to the town Kyle's job was at, which was about twelve miles from Alba. We lived there for less than a year, then moved back to Alba.

I was two months shy of being twenty years old when I found out I was going to have a baby. I was ecstatic. I didn't show excitement outwardly very often, but the excitement I felt inside when I found out the best news ever wanted to burst out of me. Kyle and I had been waiting for this day. He too, was thrilled. I loved being pregnant. As my belly grew, the reality of having a baby was the beginning of my dream in life. I was going to have the perfect family, and my happiness was overflowing.

I ate and gained at least fifty pounds, but I was happier than I had been in all my life. I began to feel her inside of me. I could not imagine a better feeling than having my little miracle inside of me. My baby would be mine always. My baby would be part of me. That part of me would be inside of her forever. My baby would always be in my life. Always.

The night came when it was time to deliver my bundle of joy. My labor was not bad. The pain was all worth getting to see my beautiful, healthy, baby girl. To see her beautiful face, her little toes, and her little fingers was better than I could have ever imagined. She had a head full of dark hair with a hint of blonde. I had my baby I had always wanted.

I had decided on a name for her already. There was a soap opera I watched, and I gave her the name of a girl on that soap. Her middle name would be after me: Tara Hope.

When Tara came home with me, I could not wait to take care of her. Her room was all fixed up with all the things she needed. The baby things my family and friends had given us for her filled her room with cheer.

Mother came home with me to help me take care of Tara. She planned to stay for two weeks. Mother held her, hugged her tight, kissed and rocked her. I couldn't help but wonder if Mother gave me that kind of affection when I was her baby girl. She would say over and over how pretty she was. It was good to have Mother there with me to help; taking care of a little baby was all new to me, but I was going to take good care of her forever.

Mother and I had become closer in the past two years. She was showing more love than I remember ever receiving from her. I needed Mother to show me love that I had known she had inside for a long time. Mother was always the most important person in my life. Kyle and Tara would be the most important to me now.

I did as I told myself I would do. I gave Tara kisses and hugs, and I told her I loved her. I felt as if I were the only one that needed to take care of all her needs. I loved Tara so much. It was a different kind of love. It was love in my heart I could not explain. My attention was on Tara only.

Having a baby was reality now. It wasn't just a dream I had as a teenager. My dream had come true for me. I had a perfect family: a daddy, a momma, and our baby. I always knew I would make it happen. I would have a great life with my family. We would have a happy home, full of love.

When Mother went home, I was ready to take on everything I was to do for Tara. It was my responsibility to make a happy life for her. Mother lived close to me, so I knew she was there for me to call and ask questions I needed to know as a new mother. She was there, now, to help me in my life. She gave me hope that I would be a good mother. She was giving me the attention that she had given the church and the people at our church. I felt I had a purpose in Mother's life now. Of course, I did all my life, but I knew it now. She was now showing her inner love by giving me affection outwardly.

I took lots of pictures of Tara to keep so she would be able to look back on all the memories. She would know how she looked as a baby growing up. There aren't many pictures that were taken of me when I was a baby; I've only seen two.

The pictures were not very clear, so I really couldn't make out how I looked. I had nothing to compare me to Tara. That's why I would make sure there were lots of pictures of her. I would have pictures to cherish from all ages of her life.

I couldn't wait to hear Tara's first word. I loved to hear her coo and smile, and hear her little laugh. I was proud to see her sit up by herself, and to see her take her first step. All these things were my rewards of being a mother. Having my baby is all I thought it would be.

I read to her. I bought her learning toys and baby dolls. I watched her play as I fixed her bottles and food. I was overjoyed to be able to stay home with her. I was able to see her take her first steps of her journey of life.

I began to talk to Kyle about building a house for us. Tara was about nine months old now. I wanted a new home for our family.

We looked at floor plans and decided how we wanted our new home to be. Kyle and I, his father, and other family members did most of the work building our home. It was all completed in about three months, and I was thrilled to have our new home. It was beautiful. The living room was big, and the kitchen was, too. There were three bedrooms and two bathrooms. Everything in my life was exactly the way I always wanted it to be.

During the day, I would play with Tara, clean the house and do the other household chores. We would go outside, and I would swing her in her tree swing. As I was swinging her, I sang to her. I rocked her and read books to her. Tara learned very quickly, and she was so eager to learn. She learned to walk when she was nine months old, and she memorized her favorite book, *Over in the Meadow,* when she was only twelve months old. Tara was a good baby, and she made me so proud.

WHAT IS WRONG WITH ME?

When Tara was fifteen months old, I found out I was going to have another baby. I began to have fears of having two babies almost immediately after the reality set in that I was going to have another one. I was scared. I didn't know what was wrong with me. I was going to have the second baby of the three or four I wanted to have. This was the way my dream in life was to happen. The perfect family I longed for did become a reality. I had my perfect family, and happiness should be surrounding me. I felt sadness, though. Would I be a failure to my baby and my family?

I could not show or speak of the fear that I held inside of me. I tried so hard to show some sign of excitement. I should be glowing with joy. Why was I so fearful? I wanted another baby, but I wasn't ready yet.

Kyle and I had talked about having another baby. I had stopped taking birth control, but I thought it would take longer than it did for me to get pregnant. My life was wonderful, but with a new baby on the way, would I be able to be a good momma to both of my babies? This worried me.

The fear and thoughts I had became worse and worse. As time went on with my pregnancy, I could not even tell myself the fears would go away. The joy, excitement and happiness I should have had were not happening. My struggle to show all of these feelings were most difficult. I was consumed with all sorts of fears that I could not take care of two babies.

I was a good momma to Tara. Could I be a good momma to my new baby? Could I be as good of a momma to my baby that was growing inside of me? I didn't see how that would be possible. Tara wasn't even two years old yet. Was she too young to have a brother or sister? I had to get Tara potty-trained. I couldn't change both of their diapers. How could I fix my new baby's bottles? I had to read to Tara. I had to play with her. I had to go outside and swing her. My fears were beginning to consume my whole being. I became much worse as the months went by.

I didn't care what I looked like anymore. I wasn't putting on make-up when I went somewhere. I sat at the house most of my days now with fearful thoughts going through my head. How would I ever be able to take good enough care of Tara? I wouldn't be able to do that and take care of my new baby, too. I just knew I would not be a good momma now.

I began to do just the necessities for Tara. I made sure she was fed. I made sure she had her bath. She played mostly by herself now. I couldn't even make myself play with her. It was hard for me to read to her. All the things I loved doing with Tara seemed to almost cease. What was Tara thinking in her mind? Was she wondering what was wrong with her momma?

I was about seven months along in my pregnancy and I didn't want to leave my house at all any more. I just didn't feel like doing anything. I didn't want to see or talk to anyone.

I did manage to go to the grocery store. I went to my doctor's appointments. I cooked supper. I didn't clean the house as much any more. I just wanted to crawl in bed and stay there. I did sleep whenever I got the opportunity. My doctor told me my baby was growing, and she was fine. I could not even be excited.

I continually told myself I was not going to be able to take care of my babies. How could I love my babies equally? Would I give them the attention and love they needed? I didn't know if I could do that. I wouldn't be a good momma anymore. I thought, "I can't take care of my baby and Tara, too." That was going to be too difficult. I wouldn't be able to handle it. The one thing in life I always wanted was to be a mother, and I was going to be a failure. I knew I would be.

As time got closer to my due date, I became even more and more scared to have my baby. My thoughts of being a horrible momma would not go away. All the fears of how I would not be able to take care of my babies would not go away. Someone else would have to take care of my babies. I couldn't do it. I was convinced I would not be able to.

I was afraid someone would come to my house to see me. They would see I wasn't the same person they knew. I didn't want to be around anybody. Please don't let anyone knock on my door. I panicked if the phone rang. I wanted to be all alone. Tara was the only one who needed me. Everyone else did not need to see me or talk to me. I definitely did not want to talk to anyone. I didn't know what to say.

It was difficult to be around my family and friends. I didn't want them to know these thoughts in my head. I couldn't tell them I wasn't going to be able to take care of my babies. I had to keep all of this to myself. If I avoided them, maybe they wouldn't figure out something was wrong with me. They wouldn't see how horrible I looked. I couldn't let anyone know of all my fears. I had to keep everyone from knowing something was wrong with me. I didn't know what was happening to me. It was horrible.

My babies would only be two years apart. It was too soon to have another baby. I would be the worst momma ever.

I tried to fix up the new baby's room. I tried to get everything prepared for her. I could not imagine bringing my baby home when her momma would not be able to take care of her.

The night came when I went into labor. I waited until I knew I had to go to the hospital to have my baby. I started spotting blood. Why was I doing this? I didn't do that with Tara. Was something bad going to happen? My pain was getting worse. I had to hurry and get to the hospital. My baby was going to come soon, and I had to be strong. I couldn't let anyone know of the fears I had been having all these months. I kept thinking of how I was going to take care of my baby I was about to bring into this world. I wouldn't know how to do anything for her. I knew someone would have to take care of her. I definitely could not do it. I didn't know how to take care of her. This I knew was true. I had these thoughts every day for the entire time I was pregnant, and they did not go away.

Kyle stopped at his Mother's house to pick her up to ride with us to the hospital. I was having strong contractions, and I knew we had to get to the hospital as fast as we could. Finally, I was at the hospital. I was dilated to eight centimeters. The nurses were saying I had to be prepped right away. Then I heard someone say "We've got to take her to the delivery room." I heard these things they were saying, but the reality of all this happening wasn't there. I lay there with very little emotion.

I had another healthy, beautiful, baby girl. She looked identical to Tara when she was born. She was a bigger baby than Tara was. Her hair was the same color as Tara's when she was born. Just as I had named Tara after a girl on a soap opera, I named the new baby after a girl from a soap opera too. Kyle chose her middle name, so our newborn baby was named Kayla Shae.

How could a mother be so afraid even to touch her baby? I was a horrible mother. I was terrified to hold my baby. I didn't know how too. I wouldn't hold her head up right. There was no way I could feed her. I couldn't change her diaper. I didn't know how to do any of these things for my baby. All through my pregnancy, I kept telling myself I would not be able to take care of my new baby. She was here now, and I couldn't do anything for her. I would do everything all wrong. It was reality now. I had my baby now, and the fears were still with me. They were even worse now that my baby was here. Still, no one knew of all my fears or how I felt. I didn't know how to explain it all to them. I didn't even understand myself what was wrong with me.

I lost quite a bit of blood during the delivery. They had to put a catheter in me this time. The nurse brought Kayla to my room so I could hold her and feed her. I thought, "What do I do? I can't do anything. I cannot pick up my baby and hold her, much less feed her. I wouldn't do anything right with her. "I pushed the call button for the nurse to come.

"Could you come get my baby?" I asked. "Since I have this catheter in me, I can't pick her up." I was hoping she wouldn't think I was a bad mother. The problem wasn't the catheter. My problem was I could not make myself reach over and pick my baby up. I didn't want them to make me feed her and take care of her.

The nurse just needed to take my baby. They knew how to hold her and feed her. They could change her diaper, because I couldn't do that, either. I was not a good momma. Why couldn't I be? What was wrong with me? I was afraid to do anything for my baby. I was afraid to hold her in my arms. The nurse picked Kayla up. She cuddled her and talked to her. Why couldn't I do that? I was so sad, but there were no tears. I was totally numb to it all.

When I had Tara, I was the one that did everything for her. No one needed to help me with Tara. However, Kayla did need someone else to take care of her. Her momma couldn't do it. I did manage to get her dressed the day we were to take her home. As the nurse wheeled me to the car, I was holding her in my arms. I could hardly smile at my baby. What was going to happen now?

I was very depressed, and I didn't even realize it. I didn't know anything about depression. No one I knew had ever talked about it. I didn't have a clue that this was why I felt the way I did. Depression had taken over me and consumed my whole being.

Mother came home with me as she had done when I brought Tara home from the hospital after I had her. Thank God, she was going to be there to do everything for Kayla. Mother would have to do all of it. She had to.

Mother held Kayla close to her. She rocked her and talked to her, just as she had done with Tara. She fixed her bottles and fed her. She changed her diapers and laid her down to sleep. I would just sit and watch Mother take care of Kayla, and she was so good to Kayla; she took care of Kayla's every need. I was not good enough for Kayla or Tara now.

Mother slept in Kayla's room. She got up in the middle of the night with Kayla. I would lie in my bed knowing my mother was taking care of my baby. I knew Kayla was all right as long as Mother took care of her. How did Mother know what to do? I didn't know.

A few days went by. I was still sitting. I was not able to convince myself I could do anything for Kayla. I could not even do anything for myself. I kept my pajamas and housecoat on all day almost every day. I wasn't brushing my teeth or brushing my hair. I was in a daze. I was in my own world without any feelings. I didn't cry. I didn't say anything about being fearful. I didn't know what was going on with me. I rarely said anything at all.

I wasn't even thinking of Tara. It was as if I had forgotten about her. She wasn't in the world I was in now. No one was, other than Mother and Kayla. I continued to watch Mother take care of Kayla. I felt as I did as a child. I was looking through that window again. I was seeing everything around me happening. I couldn't be as perfect as Mother was. This time I didn't want to be on the other side of the window. I was safe on the other side looking in. I didn't care if Mother thought I was good or not; I knew I wasn't good for anything now.

I didn't know how many days it had been since I brought Kayla home. I had no concept of time. The days just ran together. My fears and my bad thoughts were with me continuously. I kept telling myself I could not do anything, and I thought I would be this way forever.

I would freeze when Kayla cried at night. I was always awake. My sleep became nightmares and cold sweats. I shivered and shook. I wanted daylight to come. The nightmares would go away when daylight came. I didn't shiver and shake during the day. The cold sweats would go away. I hated the nighttime. When it was daytime, I could sit and watch Mother taking care of Kayla. At least I wasn't as restless as I was in bed in the dark. My thought of not being a good mother was still in my head every day. I would sit in sadness and numbness thinking of how horrible all this was. I can't change back to the good momma I had been for Tara. I wasn't a good momma for Tara or Kayla.

Kyle and I didn't have much conversation at all between us now. I didn't know how long it had been since we had talked to each other. He never asked what was wrong with me. Our communication seemed to cease. He came home from work and ate the supper Mother had made. Afterwards, he sat in the living room and watched TV. I didn't pay any attention to what he was doing; I didn't even acknowledge his presence. I don't know how he felt about all of this. I don't know if he was even aware at night that I lay in bed shaking.

Mother was getting ready to give Kayla a bath one day. We were in the bathroom together. Mother was filling the bathroom sink with water, getting the water just the right temperature. I just stood beside her and watched.

Mother said to me, "You give Kayla her bath."

What! Please no! Don't make me do that. I immediately thought I would hurt Kayla. I was afraid I would hit her head on the sink. I could not take the chance of possibly dropping her. I didn't want to harm Kayla. I just didn't know how to hold her head up carefully.

I just looked at Mother and nodded and said to her, "You do it, Mother." She didn't say anything to me. You know how to do it. That's what I wanted to say to her. Mother bathed Kayla as I watched.

I could only watch Mother. I couldn't help her in any way. I no longer had that instinct of knowing what to do as a mother. Didn't anyone understand? I could not be a mother. I didn't know how to anymore. I wasn't able to do all the things mothers do for their babies without even thinking of it. It's supposed to come naturally, but it wasn't for me.

I couldn't fix her bottles. I didn't know how much milk to put in them. If I tried to give her a bottle, I might spill the milk all over her face, and she could drown. I didn't know how to hold her to feed her a bottle. I wouldn't try to. I would not take Kayla in my arms. Something bad would happen to her if she were in my arms.

When would I feel better, or would I? Would I ever be able to take care of my baby? I didn't think I ever would. The same thoughts kept racing in my mind, and they were horrible thoughts.

The reality of becoming a Mother again certainly did not sit well with me. I was a failure at the one thing I wanted to be in my life. My perfect family was crumbling apart. I could not be the perfect wife, or the perfect mother. I could not accomplish trying to be perfect anymore. I was just a horrible person. Nobody needed me at all. My babies would be better off without me.

I was getting worse as the days went by. I don't know how long it had been since I had taken a bath. I didn't know how long it had been since I had eaten something. Every day was the same. I had not had a good day in a very, very long time. In fact, it had been months since I had felt happy.

One day when I was just sitting on the couch, Mother said to me, "Melody, why don't you go take a bath."

Oh, no. I don't know if I can. I went into the bathroom. I stared at the bathtub. I looked at the faucets. Which faucet was for the cold water? Which was for the hot water? I started to reach for one of the faucets. I couldn't do it. I couldn't even run my bath water. I don't know how long I stood in the bathroom. I walked out. I didn't take a bath.

Mother had started to get agitated with me. She wanted me to take my responsibility and take care of my baby.

She raised her voice at me and said, "You need to take care of Kayla!"

Then she said to me, "You took care of Tara; you did everything for Tara."

What should I do? I felt so bad, but I felt worse knowing she might make me do everything for Kayla all by myself. The reality hit me. Mother was just staying for a short time. She was going to go home.

I was lying in my bed. The cold sweats came. The nightmares came. I began thinking about what I had heard on TV that night. I wasn't watching TV, I had just heard the commentator telling about a mother who had put her baby in the oven. Oh, my gosh! Was I that kind of mother? Would I put Kayla in the oven? I lay there tossing and turning, wanting these thoughts in my head to go away.

My forehead and chest were wet from sweating. My heart was pounding. The worst fear washed over me. How could I think like that? I couldn't lie there any longer.

I went in Kayla's room where she and Mother were sleeping.

"Mother," I said softly, but in complete fear, "this woman put her baby in the oven." I was horrified. I didn't want to believe it.

I knelt down beside Mother and whispered, "Mother, this woman is a bad Mother. A bad Mother like me." Mother just lay there. Did she know what I was telling her? Was this a nightmare? Was this real? How could a mother do that to her baby? I went back to bed shivering. Please, let daylight come. I can't stand this.

When morning came, I thought about that woman and what she had done to her baby. I didn't know if it was true, or if, in fact, it was a nightmare. It was daytime now. The night was over. The worst time of the day was my nights. I was not going to think about that. It couldn't be true. I would never do that to Kayla. I knew that. My thoughts of what that mother did went away, and I didn't think about it again.

I thought about God. Where is God? I desperately needed him now. When I tried to pray, I could barely get "Dear God" out of my mouth. I couldn't even pray anymore. I'd hang my head in my hands. I would yell out in my head, "God! God! Oh, please help me! Help me!"

The day came when Mother had to go home. I was scared out of my mind. She could not go. She could not leave me here alone with Kayla. What would happen? What was I going to do? I hadn't been able to do anything for Kayla all this time. I was not a good mother or a good person. How could I tell Mother I could not take care of Kayla? It had been about two weeks now since I had come home from the hospital after having Kayla.

Mother was leaving. I followed her to her car, and I pleaded with her, "Please stay a little longer."

"Melody, you're fine," Mother said with assurance.

Mother didn't have a clue how I felt. My grandmother, Nonnie, had been sick, and Mother was going to go check on her. I didn't care that she needed to go see Nonnie. She was my Mother, and I needed her. She didn't realize how much I needed her to stay.

Mother got in her car and told me bye. She was gone. I panicked and ran inside my house. I looked at Kayla's bottles on the kitchen counter. They were going to have to be washed and filled. What do I do? I was like a lost child. I needed my mother.

I sat down at my kitchen table facing the clock on the wall. I watched the clock in front of me. This must have been the first time in two weeks I had even looked at the clock. The seconds went by. The minutes went by. I didn't take my eyes off the clock. I knew how long it took Mother to get home. The time came. She would be home now. The time had come to call Mother. I picked up the phone and dialed her phone number. The phone rang and rang. I was not going to hang up.

"Hello." It was Mother.

"You've got to come back, Mother. I need you here, please." I was pleading with Mother again.

I didn't even acknowledge anything Mother was saying. I just kept telling her, "I need you; please, come back."

Then Mother said, "I'll be there as soon as I can."

A big sigh of relief came out of me. She was coming back.

I sat still waiting for her. I didn't think about Kayla. I just sat in the chair. Mother finally got to my house. She brought my sister, Debbie, with her. They weren't there for very long before Debbie called my gynecologist. She told him what was going on with me and he said it was post-partum blues. But Debbie knew it was much worse than post-partum blues. I had been depressed months before I had Kayla. Before she hung up the phone, my doctor recommended that an appointment be made for me to go see a psychiatrist.

Afterwards, Mother and Debbie were talking, and Mother said, "There's nothing wrong with Melody. She doesn't need to go see a psychiatrist."

Needing a psychiatrist was unheard of unless you were crazy. Mother would not admit that I needed that kind of help.

"Mother, Melody is depressed. She can't help it," Debbie said to Mother.

"Melody is not getting better. She's got to have some help," Debbie said, convincing Mother.

Debbie was letting Mother know what had to be done. Debbie had suffered through a state of depression in her life some years back. She didn't tell anyone until years later. She could see all the signs of it in me.

I just listened to them. I didn't say a word. It didn't register with me what was about to happen.

The next thing I knew, I was riding in the car with Mother and Debbie, and I didn't know where we were going. We pulled up to the doctor's office.

We went in, and I sat down in a chair. I was given papers to fill out. There were so many questions to answer. Do you feel sad? Yes. Do you sleep well? No. Do you want to be alone? No. Yes. The questions went on and on. I was trying to figure out what the right answers were. I had to be answering them all wrong. As I read on, I thought, "something is definitely wrong with me." What was going to happen to me? The doctor could not know all this. I was not crazy, or was I? I hadn't been able to tell anyone my thoughts because I knew they would think I was crazy. Now they were all going to know I was.

As I was trying to finish answering all the questions, there were two questions I didn't know. One question was, "Does anyone in your family suffer from depression?" No. I didn't know. There was no one that I knew of that did. Another question was, "Does anyone in your family have a mental illness?" Oh my gosh. No one did. I was the only one that was this way. Everybody else was fine. My whole family was normal. I was quiet as I sat there turning page after page of these questions.

My name was called, and Mother and Debbie got up. I stood up and followed them. We all went into the doctor's office. I was not fighting this at all. Why? Was I going to be all right? Mother and Debbie would take care of all of this.

I was sitting in a chair in front of a huge man. He was tall and big. He began to talk to Mother and Debbie. I was tuning it all out. Then I heard the doctor telling them what he recommended.

The doctor offered two plans. Plan A and plan B.

"Melody can take medication," the doctor told them; "We will see if the medication will help her." This was plan A. "If it doesn't, we can admit her in to the hospital for two weeks. Melody's medication can be monitored in the hospital." So this was plan B.

Mother and Debbie decided to go with plan A. The prescriptions were given to them. We got back in the car and left. I didn't say a word to the doctor. He didn't know me. He didn't know I couldn't do anything. How did he know what to do for me? He didn't know I was not a good mother anymore. He was not aware that I could not even stand to touch my baby or take care of her. What about Tara? Tara entered my mind now.

The only words I could think about his saying were, "she needs medication," or "she may need to be hospitalized." Mother and Debbie had done all the talking. Did anyone care to talk to me, or ask me questions? I had tried to answer the pages of questions I was given when I walked in that place. That was all I did. They had decided what was going to happen to me.

The reality of knowing what I was going to do now had not sunk in. I followed Mother and Debbie. I did what they told me to do. My focus was all on them. I wasn't thinking about what I should do. I was clinging to Mother and Debbie, too. I still could not get any words to come out of my mouth to explain how I felt. I still could not do anything on my own. I had been relying on Mother all this time. Now it was Mother and Debbie, too; I was relying on them both. Now both of them would make sure I wasn't alone. They could do everything for Kayla. They needed to understand I could not do anything. They need to understand that I am not a good mother.

From the beginning of my pregnancy with Kayla, my fears had consumed my whole being. My thoughts had convinced me I couldn't be the mother Tara and Kayla needed. How could I take care of two babies? I had to give them love and attention equally. Was that possible? No. It wasn't possible for me to accomplish that. I became a mother who wouldn't be able to care for my babies. I gave in to all my fears. I could not overcome them. My mind was not functioning right. My body was barely functioning now. I was weak. My inward strength and outward strength was no longer there. It hadn't been there all this time.

Mother came back to my home to stay with me a while longer. I never thought of what Mother was going through. Mother was strong, as she had always been. I didn't realize how this must have been hurting her inside. She was right by my side. I needed her even more now than ever.

Mother gave me my medicine every day. I began to slip further away. I just wanted to die now. My faith and hope were gone. I just had to die. I didn't want to be this way anymore. I wanted out of my misery. I had no reason to live now. I had to go. Someone else had to take care of Tara and Kayla. I was not any good for them. They would be better off without me. Tara and Kayla would be happier with someone else. Someone else could take care of them; I couldn't. I wanted to go away and leave them in good hands.

I made sure Mother stood by me every time I took my medicine. I wanted to take all of the medicine I had all at once. I would die then, and this would be all over. I made sure she watched me take my medicine, because, inside of me, I knew Mother would not let me swallow all the pills at once. There was a part of me that didn't want to die, but I knew it would be the best thing for my girls and everyone else.

I didn't tell Mother I wanted to die. It was wrong to think that. She would know I was crazy. I couldn't stay here. I couldn't be a good mother, and that was what I lived for. I had to leave my girls behind. I couldn't be a part of their lives. They deserved someone better.

Kyle and I hadn't said much of anything to each other since we brought Kayla home from the hospital. I wasn't able to communicate with anyone. All I thought about was the fears I had, and wanting to die.

My Deep, Dark Hole

I am in a deep, dark hole. I have been here for several months. This is my reality now. It's very dark. I'm all alone in this hole. No one can help me. My emotions are gone. There is absolutely no hope to be found here. My tears will not fall on my face.

I want out of my darkness. I'm fearful. I will never overcome this. I can not even pick one foot up to begin to climb out of this hole. I'm so far down there's no sight of light. I don't want to live here. I need to get out. I want to die. I can not stay here. No one understands. They don't know what is in my head—all the horrible thoughts.

I keep the thoughts inside my head. I can't tell anyone that I can't hold my baby. I can't comfort my baby. I can't touch her. I will do everything all wrong. I can't do it!

Doesn't everyone know this? How can they? How can they not? I won't talk. I cannot share my thoughts with anyone. I've got to go to the place my pills are. I need to pour them all out of the bottle into my hand. I must take all of them. I cannot be here in this life.

Kayla, my baby; Tara my little girl, I will. I will go. I will die. Someone else can make my girls happy. Their momma can't do it. Their momma can't give them the hugs and the kisses. I can't say the words. "I love you." My girls are better off without me. I am not a good momma. No one can tell me I am. I can't find the mother inside of me. I don't know how I got in this hole. There is no way out.

There is much pain in my heart. I am miserable. I am sad. I am just existing now. All the feelings I'm supposed to have have been gone for so long. I don't know how to get them back. I am a failure. There is only despair. I am not good. I am not good.

My thoughts are making me dig deeper into my dark hole. There is not one good thought inside me. I want to die.

Debbie came back to my house because I had not gotten any better. She was calling the psychiatrist again. I was much worse, now. The medication that was given to me had not helped me. Mother and Debbie did the only thing they knew to do. They had to try Plan B.

I was admitted to the same hospital where I had Tara two years ago, and then had had Kayla two weeks ago. This time I was in a different place in the hospital. I was in the psychiatric ward. This is where crazy people come, I'm thinking. I am out of my mind. I am crazy. I am a person no one understands.

I was checked in. I went to a room and the first bed in the room would be mine. In the other bed was an older lady. She looked to be the age of a grandmother. I was left there to stay. I didn't know what would happen from here. I was terrified of the unknown.

I lay in my bed the first night I was there. I was soaking up my environment. I couldn't sleep. I wanted to call Mother. I wanted morning to come. The night as always was the worse. The night is when all the horrible thoughts would go through my mind. What were they going to do to me? How long would I have to stay here? I still just wanted to die. That thought kept going through my mind, over and over.

The lady next to me stayed up all night, too. She kept the bathroom light on, and went back and forth from her bed to the bathroom. She talked to herself and sang to herself. She was in her own world, too, just as I was. The TV was on. How could I sleep with all the noise she was making? But I'm sure I wouldn't be able to sleep even if she wasn't making so much noise.

The morning finally came. A nurse came in the room and said to me, "Time to get up."

I just wanted to lie in the bed. I didn't want to leave this room. I certainly didn't want to see anybody that was here. I could not do anything when I was at home. What's different here in this psyche ward that would make me be able to do anything? Which was scarier? Being at home where I was afraid to take care of my baby, or here, with the reality that something was seriously wrong with me?

I was to get up early, make my bed, take a shower and get dressed. I didn't even do that at home. I attempted to make my bed. I couldn't take a shower. That was too difficult. There would be no shower for me today. I didn't get dressed, either.

I walked out of my room in my pajamas and housecoat. A nurse was at the end of the hall. There was a line of people in front of her, leading to the nurse to get a little paper cup filled with your pills. This was how your medication was monitored. I remember my doctor had told Mother and Debbie that my medication could be monitored in the hospital.

I took my little paper cup from the nurse. I put it to my mouth, poured my pills in, and took my small cup of water. I swallowed them and followed the line into a big room where our breakfast was served.

As I picked at my food, I observed everyone who walked in the room. Some people were dressed. Some of them were still in their pajamas and housecoats like I was. There was some that was doing the same as I was. They were just sitting there, picking at their food. Some looked so sad. This was a sad place.

Some of the people were talking amongst themselves, even laughing. How could anyone laugh? Laughing was a sound that hadn't come from me in a long time. What was next?

I didn't know what was next that day. I receded back to my own world, to my thoughts of what was going to happen to me. When would I get out of this place? I have no will to live. I am weak. I did what I was told, or as much as I could make myself do. It was so hard for me to focus long enough to do anything. I couldn't think straight for long before my mind went weary. I was very tired from all this. Let me go to my bed and stay there. I need rest. My body didn't want to move. I need to get rid of wanting to die. I want my fear of living to go away. I had lost my mind. I had definitely lost the part of my mind that made me function.

My mother-in-law had brought me some candy: M & M's. I loved M & M's. When I would lie in my bed and think of how I wanted to take all my pills so I would die, I would get a handful of my M & M's. I would pour lots of them in my hand and put them in my mouth. I thought this is what I would do if I had all my pills.

There was a phone in my room beside my bed. I would call Mother. I hated it here. I had to talk to Mother. I called her several times. They eventually took the phone out of my room because I was calling her so much.

I'm still in my dark hole. I cannot climb out. I need someone to understand and realize where I am. Please throw me a rope. Someone must pull me out. I can't get out without help. Will I be stuck here forever? Will anyone be able to figure out what is in my head? I don't know how to tell them.

The night came again. It was another night next to the crazy lady in my room. How do I get through all of this? Why can't I just scream out loud or cry? Who am I now? Melody is gone.

Mother came to see me, I told her all about the crazy lady. I finally told her one of the many fears I had. This crazy lady next to me gave my room an eerie feeling. What was wrong with her?

The next morning, I woke up to the same routine of this psyche ward. Get out of bed, make my bed, and take a shower. Nope, I still couldn't take a shower.

Get dressed. Stand in line. Take my pills. Go in the room to eat with so many people. I can't eat. Maybe I'll have just a few bites. I hate this!

Did everyone here feel like I did? Were they in their own dark holes? It didn't seem like all of them were. Some were dressed nicely, and even had their socks and shoes on. There were women who actually had on make-up. They had brushed and fixed their hair. Were they going somewhere? I could barely make myself get out of bed.

My friends, Tracy and Delaine, come to see me and were talking as we walked down the hallway. I wasn't paying much attention to what they were saying. I was thinking of how embarrassed I was for them to see me this way.

I had just had my baby two weeks ago. Was it two weeks ago or was it a month ago? I don't know. Some lady told me I didn't look like I had just a baby. Did I tell her I had a baby? I didn't remember telling anyone I had. Did the lady not believe I had a baby recently? I knew I had a baby. I'm not so crazy I had forgotten my baby. I just couldn't be with her right now because I couldn't take care of her. Would I ever be able to? I didn't have much weight left on me. I had lost most of what I had gained with my baby. Could that be why the lady told me I didn't look like I had just had a baby?

I went back to my room and found that the lady who had been in the room with me was gone. I felt such relief. Mother had told them to get her out of there. She must have.

The next day I had a different roommate. She looked to be younger than I, though I was only twenty-two. There didn't seem to be anything wrong with her. She was pretty and she talked a lot—to me—not to herself. I liked her. I was glad she had come.

I listened to every word she was saying to me. She was telling me her story. She knew exactly what to do about it too. I could see her pain and anger. She was strong, though, unlike me.

She was telling me about her boyfriend. They were having problems. She had overdosed and was brought here, where they had pumped her stomach. I couldn't help but wonder what would have happened to me if I had taken my pills as I had wanted to. She told me she was not going to be kept here.

"I will get out. I will not stay here," she said with total determination.

I felt somewhat safe that night with her in my room. She gave me hope that I could be strong, and her determination flowed from her to me. For the first time since I had begun to slip further and further in my dark hole, there was hope that I could climb out now.

I knew I had to do it by myself. There was no one who could drop the rope for me to be pulled out. I had to climb out, just as I had slipped away, down deep into it. This had to be my decision to come out and face my fears. I had to want to come out. I was still tired. I was going to fight back my fears. I did want to live. I would survive and live my life with no fear.

I began to remember that Tara and Kayla were home. They had been pushed back in my mind. The fears had taken over all my thoughts of going home to them. I wanted to go home to my girls. They needed me, and I needed them desperately. I wanted to hold Kayla and rock her in my arms. I had to hug Tara and let her know her momma came back to read to her and play with her. To be with Tara and Kayla is all I wanted. I was going to bring back the mother I once was. I had to get back to the most important people in my life. After all, being a mother is what I was going to be when I grew up. I was grown now, and I was a mother, with the most beautiful girls in the world. I will take care of Tara and Kayla, now. I was beginning to believe now I would do just that. It felt so wonderful inside to have emotions coming back.

One day some of us in the psyche ward went in to a room with a long table in the middle of it. There were chairs all around the table. Each one of us picked a chair and sat down. I guess this was our therapy. This particular day, I broke down and cried while I listened to a girl that looked to be around my age. She was talking about when her daddy had died. This triggered memories of the day my daddy died. She told us she was a young teenager when it happened. I could relate to how she felt; I was a young teenager when my Daddy had died too. She cried as she told us about it, and it made me sad. I actually did have emotions: I was crying.

"Melody, are you all right?" the head lady of this therapy asked.

I nodded; I was not going to say a word. Just let me leave this room. I was not going to share my thoughts, no way.

A little while later after we left the therapy room, a nurse came up to me and said, "Melody, your doctor is here to see you."

It's not time for my doctor to be here. Why was he here?

I went in a small room. My huge doctor was sitting in a big chair, and I sat down in the other chair that was facing him. Since the first time I saw him, I didn't like him. I didn't want to be in this room with him.

With his deep voice that made me cringe, he said, "I understand you cried today."

"Yes," I said quietly.

I didn't want to look at him. I was furious. Is it all right for me to cry? Did I do something wrong? This was a big breakthrough for me. I had thought of someone else's pain. It made me sad hearing that girl tell her story. There was a glimpse of light for me now, though. I wasn't the only person who was suffering. Someone else had sorrow, too. It actually felt good to cry. I hadn't been able to cry in such a long time. I hadn't had any kind of emotions in a long time.

My doctor then said to me, "Maybe you're not ready to go home. We might need to keep you here a while longer."

I was getting angrier listening to what he was telling me. I didn't tell him why I had cried. He didn't ask me why, either. I just sat there in silence wanting to leave the room. Did he think I should stay longer because I had cried? What was wrong with that?

I'm climbing out of this dark hole. I was angry now. I was angry I was here. I would not stay here. I was going to fight this now. I was climbing up instead of sliding deeper into the darkness of my hole. I knew I had to get out.

I felt brave enough now to say something to my doctor. I was calm. I looked at him. "Oh, I'm feeling much better. I'm ready to go home," I said very convincingly.

I was brave, but scared. I had just lied to my doctor. I wasn't sure I felt better. I wanted to go home, but, I didn't know if I would be the same way when I left here, as I was when I came here. How would I be at home?

I was not staying in this place. I had to get out. I had observed everything here. I didn't like any part of it. I had straight-out lied to my doctor. Amazingly, he bought it. I could go home in a few more days. I wasn't going to have to stay in this dreadful place.

My psychiatrist didn't know what I had just done. I thought to myself, this man is a psychiatrist. "He is not good at his job." He still didn't know anything about me. He had not talked to me about anything. He didn't know my thoughts. This doctor was a quack. It was so easy for me to make him believe I felt better. Was I better?

Now I began to wonder what I was going to do when I went home. Could I be a good mother when I got there? I had to be. I wanted to be. I was finding the mother in me. I was thinking of my girls. I missed them.

My roommate got up the next morning, and I watched as she made her bed. After that, she gathered up her things and went out of the room. She took her clothes, her brush, her make-up bag, and her toothbrush.

I can make up my bed like she had done. I tried my best to make the bed up that day better than I had done since I had been here. I was beginning to want to show I could do it now. I believed I could.

My roommate came back in our room. There was a shower room outside our entrance door, and to the right. I could see that she had taken a shower. She was fully dressed. She even had her shoes on. She looked fresh and ready to start the day.

I began to gather my things to go to the shower room. Had I taken a shower during this whole time I had been here? Had I even brushed my teeth, or washed my hair?

I took my things into the shower room as I struggled with the thoughts of being able to turn the water on and bathe. I did it, though. What a feeling to feel clean and fresh. Fresh, like my roommate was. I put my clothes on. I had washed my hair. I brushed my teeth. These simple things had been so hard for me to do.

I went back to my room. I was ready to start my day, too. My roommate and I talked some. She inspired me to move forward.

We went into the hall and got in line to take our medication. We sat in the room where we ate. I actually felt hungry. I was eating my food, instead of just picking at it.

Before the day was over my roommate had left. She was gone. I felt there was a purpose in her coming and being with me for those couple of days. Even my faith was coming back to me. I was thankful to God, now. He had been with me all this time. I realized I had forgotten him, but he had not forgotten me. I had always known that from the time I was a young girl that God was with me in good times and bad. He had always helped me to keep my faith and know Jesus was in my heart. My life was turning around, now. I had good and happy thoughts again.

I felt in my heart that the girl who had come and stayed and talked to me was an angel sent from God. She showed me courage, strength, determination, and, most of all, that there was hope for me after all. I wanted to leave here, too, and I would.

I now realized that there are angels sent from God. This girl was an angel through whom God sent his message to me. Angels are someone we meet that gives us inspiration and hope. She had shown me what I needed to see and known to guide me through the situation I was in. I was thankful I had met her.

Going Home

Everyone in the psyche ward had his or her own story. I didn't know why everyone had ended up here. I had my story that would stay with me forever, but I never shared it with anyone. I didn't even share it with my family or my doctor. I didn't tell them of all the thoughts I had battled for almost a year.

Christmas would soon be here. Many people were going to be able to go home. I was one of them. I was able to leave after two weeks, which was the time my doctor had suggested I stay.

I had had Kayla on November nineteenth. A month or a little more had passed by. I had not been able to give and show my love to Kayla yet.

Again, I didn't have that feeling a mother should feel when she came into this world. I had no excitement or joy when Kayla came. I felt so horrible that I was not able to take care of her, but I would do it now. Nothing would stop me from being a good mother now.

I was going home to touch Kayla, hold her, feed her, and be her momma. Tara was there, and she would have her momma back, too. I felt joy in my heart. At last I could not wait to see my girls. I still had fears, but there was so much less fear now.

I had come a long way. I had lost that year of my life falling and ending up in my deep, dark hole of severe depression. I hoped I would never fall back again.

The day was here now. My belongings were all packed, and I was going home. I would give my babies hugs and kisses, and tell them I loved them. I had put all the pieces back together in my head. The darkness was gone, and the light was beginning to shine through.

Kyle came to see me throughout my stay here, and, on this day he had come to take me home. After all this time, he had stayed with me. I don't know how he felt about all this. We never had talked about it.

As Kyle and I walked out of the hospital, we paused before we crossed the street to get to our car. I had a horrible thought. I thought I could walk in the middle of the road, and a car would run over me. I had one last fear. For a brief moment, thinking of going home to all my responsibilities, I thought I could still end my life. Would I be normal now and be the person I was before all this happened to me? Would I be able to take care of all my responsibilities when I got home?

I held tight to Kyle's hand as we walked across the street together. I was brave and strong and I told myself, "You can do it." I had overcome all the fears that had taken over me. I was not going to let them come back in my head.

When we got in the car and drove away from the hospital, I was all right. I couldn't wait to go home and open the door back to my life. I was full of life again. I was actually happy. The burden that had weighed so heavily on me lifted.

We drove up to our home, and I got out of the car and went to the door. I opened that door with total confidence that I could do it all again. I was a wife, a mother, a daughter, a sister, and a friend. I soaked in everything around me. I was home, and it was great! Inside of me, I was jumping and laughing and twirling in joy and happiness.

Tara! Kayla! Momma's here! I felt as if I had become a mother for the first time. I cannot explain what I was feeling. I was so thankful to be home with my family again.

Being a mother came back to me easily. I was finally taking care of Tara and Kayla. I was there to take care of all their needs. I didn't even have to think about what I was doing; it came naturally. I didn't have to think about what my next move was. I really was normal again. I wasn't crazy after all.

I was getting everything all together for Christmas. I was shopping, wrapping presents, and putting Christmas decorations up. This was the greatest Christmas I could ever remember.

I was still taking my medication and going to see my doctor. I went to see him for the first time after getting out of the hospital. I walked in his office, and the look he had on his face was as if he couldn't believe it was me. I was dressed nicely, my hair had been cut, and I looked so much better. I had make-up and a smile on my face.

When I walked in his office, he said, "You look good."

I was out of my deep, dark hole and living my life again. The light was bright now. I was out of total darkness.

MY DEEP, DARK HOLE

DO YOU SEE THAT DEEP DARK HOLE

THAT'S WHERE I WAS A FEW YEARS AGO

A PLACE DIFFICULT FOR MY SOUL

I COULD SEE NO SIGHT OF LIGHT

I STRUGGLED A LONG HARD FIGHT

THE HARDEST WAS MY NIGHT

THAT HOLE WAS FAR FROM GOOD

A PLACE I WOULD LEAVE IF ONLY I COULD

UNTIL AT LAST I KNEW I WOULD

GOD WAS MY LIGHT THAT SHINED EVERYDAY

HE GAVE ME STRENGTH I CAN SAY

AND NOW I KNOW A MUCH BETTER WAY

LIVING MY DREAM

I was still a housewife. Being at home with my girls was still just what I wanted. I wanted to be home with Kayla and Tara every day. I was a good mother.

I was still taking medication. I had no thought of taking all of them anymore. I took just what was prescribed to me. However, my medication had made me gain weight, and I didn't like it. I had always been thin. But it was all right having more weight on me than I was used to. I was feeling so much better. I was myself again. That's what mattered.

After about six months, I was able to stop taking my anti-depressant and my pill for anxiety. I didn't have any more appointments with my psychiatrist. That was all behind me now.

Tara and Kayla were growing. They were more beautiful every day. I loved watching them play and laugh. They were happy, and that made me happy. I was so proud to have them. God had blessed me tremendously.

I began to want to take them to church. They needed to know about God. They needed to know, too, that Jesus would come into their hearts. Tara was four years old, and Kayla was one. I had to get them in a church now. I had only taken them to church a few times. I felt badly that I had not taken them to church regularly. Kyle stayed home while we went to church on Sunday mornings.

The gift that Mother gave to me I had to give to Tara and Kayla. They needed me to give them the gift of learning about Jesus, just as Mother made sure I received it. The Bible stories, the singing, the people that were so loving at a church. They would learn all of these things early in their life, too, as I did.

This is where they would receive faith, hope, and love to help them through their journey of life.

I found the church I wanted to go to. I didn't go every Sunday and Sunday night. I rarely went on Wednesday night. I wasn't as faithful as Mother always had been.

Tara and Kayla heard and learned the songs that taught them Jesus loved them. "Jesus Loves Me," and "He's Got the Whole World in His Hands," along with other ones. They sang, making a joyful noise. And as they sang, I felt overwhelming joy inside.

After a short time of going to church, I began to take my girls less and less often. I soon stopped going at all, although it made me feel good when I went. It was spiritual, the songs we sang were very uplifting, and I could feel the Holy Spirit as I sang and listened to the preacher. But going to church now just didn't seem to fit in my routine.

I had a daily routine. I would get up in the morning and fix the girls breakfast. After they ate breakfast, they would play together. I would wash dishes, wash clothes, fold clothes, and do whatever housework needed to be done. At twelve o'clock or so, I would fix the girls lunch. I had a little table in the kitchen that was just for them where they ate. After they ate their lunch, I put them down for a nap. While the girls were sleeping, I would watch my soaps. This was my time. When they got up from their nap, we would all play. They would sit at their little table and play with play dough, or cut paper sacks, or draw and color. When it was warm outside, we would go out and they would play as I watched them. They would play in the water hose and make mud pies. It was great to be with them and to watch them play. I loved watching them learn and do new things. We had fun and there was much laughter.

Tara was the quite one. She soaked up everything around her. She was mature for her age, but petite in size. Her thick, dark, blonde hair was long with relaxed ringlets. Her eyes were blue with curled-up eyelashes. She was never loud or rambunctious, and she was extremely eager to learn.

Kayla was the bubbly one. Her hair was dark blonde like her sister's, but straight and silky. She had blue eyes that always twinkled. When she walked in a room, everyone knew it. She liked to be the center of attention. She was always smiling.

They both had their own personalities and different ways in which they reacted to things. They were very good girls—very well behaved. I loved them both the same. I remembered the time when I didn't know how I could love them equally.

Tara and Kayla would remember growing up together since they were only two years apart. I didn't remember my sisters, Debbie and Teresa, being with me much when I was a little girl. My sisters left home before I had a chance to share my feelings with them. I had thought when I found out I was having another baby, it was too soon. I wasn't ready for it yet. Now I was glad they were close in age. They would always play together. As they grew older, they would have someone to talk to. They could share their feelings with each other. They wouldn't feel alone.

I wanted to make sure as their mother, that I would always be there for them. My mother was there with me when I was growing up, but I didn't feel she took time to listen to me. She didn't show excitement for me, and we didn't share many laughs together. She didn't seem to ever be concerned when I was sad or if I had a bad day. Maybe, it was because she didn't know when I was sad. I didn't express myself. Now that I am older, I realize Mother showed her love very differently. She took care of me and worked hard to provide for me. Although we didn't share many mother-daughter times, I knew she loved me with all her heart. She had been there for me in many ways.

I would always comfort my girls. I would sit down with my girls and listen to their stories. I would let them know they could talk to me about anything. I would want to see their grades in school, and I would praise them when they did well. I would tell them they were pretty. I would tell them they could be anything they wanted to be. I would let them know their mother wanted to help them when they needed it. I wanted to make them happy when they felt sad. I would hug them when they were hurt. I would do all the things a mother should do and say to my girls.

When it got close to the time for Tara and Kayla's daddy to come home from work in the evening, I would start to cook supper. Tara and Kayla would sit in the floor in front of the TV and watch their favorite afternoon shows, *Sesame Street* and *Mr. Rogers*. Their shows came on at the perfect time. I could cook supper with very little interruption.

When Kyle came home, we ate supper together. Tara and Kayla sat at their little table, and Kyle and I would sit at the kitchen bar. After supper, I cleaned the kitchen, and then put Tara and Kayla in the bath. They played with their toys in the bathtub and got fresh and clean. I would get them out of the bathtub, wrap them up in towels, and they would run to the living room. They would get their pajamas on, and we would all spend some time after supper in the living room. Kyle and I would watch some TV while the girls played for a little while. Kyle would sit on the floor and play with them. After that, it was time to tuck the girls in bed.

The next morning, we would start our daily routine again. We went to the grocery store and Wal-Mart at the beginning of each month since Kyle got paid only once a month. I didn't take Tara and Kayla too many places during the week. We would go to their MeMaw's, my mother-in law, and visit with her sometimes. I loved spending my days with Tara and Kayla. I was fortunate to be able to stay home with my girls and not have to work.

On the weekends, I would sometimes go shopping with my friends to the stores in the town where I had lived as a child. I was very close to them, and I enjoyed spending time with them.

Kyle's and my friends were couples that we had gone to high school with. We all had married our high school sweethearts. My husband played softball, and so did my friend's husbands. We all went to the ball games.

Since Alba was such a small town, there wasn't a whole lot to do. We spent time with our friends at one of our houses on weekends sometimes. We would play cards, or forty-two with dominoes. We had fun just hanging out.

My life was finally perfect. I had my perfect family. I had good friends. I was so thankful for my girls. My family had a daddy, a momma, and two precious children. We had a beautiful house. It was all just as I had wanted as a young girl. I was the housewife, and I did my chores around the house and spent my days with Tara and Kayla. Kyle worked hard and provided for all of us.

My dream of having a perfect home had come true, and now I was living my dream.

I was twenty-four years old now. Tara was four years old, and Kayla was two. They had learned to sit up, walk, carry on conversations, and so many other things. There were no bottles to fix; no more changing diapers. My girls were growing up so fast. I enjoyed being a stay at home Mom and a housewife, but I began to think about getting a job.

My sister-in-law worked at a local Mexican restaurant and told me she was quitting, so I decided to go and talk to the owners about working there. They hired me, and I would be working part-time. Kyle didn't mind that I had gotten a job, and I thought it would be good for me to get out of the house some.

I knew a lady that lived close by, and she kept children at her home. She was a very sweet lady, and I knew the girls would enjoy staying there. I wouldn't worry about them because they would be in good hands.

I really liked my job and I was good it, and that made me feel good about myself. I had been working at my job for several months, when one night I went to work and thought I heard someone say I wasn't fast enough, or that I wasn't doing a good job, or something along those lines. I became very upset. It was very busy that night, and we all had to work fast to get the orders out. It wasn't that big of a deal, but I blew it all out of proportion. I got so mad I left my job and didn't go back. I just walked out and quit. When I told Kyle I had quit my job, he didn't have much to say about it. We rarely ever discussed things.

The next day or two I thought, why did I do that? I liked my job very much. The owners of the restaurant were really nice to me. I enjoyed working with them and all the other people I worked with there.

I was an easy-going person. I always tried to be nice and friendly to everyone. I didn't want to make anybody mad. I didn't want to hurt anyone's feelings. This was the type of person I always wanted to be—a good person. I felt bad for walking out on the people I worked for. They had been good to me.

I began to think people were saying bad things about me behind my back. I started thinking my friends were, too. I kept telling myself they weren't. I loved my friends. They loved me, too. I was becoming unable to convince myself that people did like me.

I started spending money we didn't have. I spent money to the point that my husband and I were overdrawn at the bank. I was writing hot checks, but the bank where we had our account covered all the checks I wrote. Kyle never questioned me about paying our bills or spending money. I had always managed our money. I had managed my money since I was fifteen years old. I had gotten us in a bind, and Kyle didn't even know it. I wouldn't tell him; I couldn't. I was afraid to. He probably would have been upset, of course, but he wouldn't have yelled and screamed at me about it or anything else. Kyle and I rarely argued. If one of us got upset about something, the other one didn't know. If we had any words, we would never yell or scream or cuss at each other. Kyle was very laid-back. Nothing ever seemed to upset him.

I spent Kyle's whole month's salary even before his next paycheck. This went on for a few months. Then there was a phone call from the bank one day. I had put us in this situation. I didn't know what to say to Kyle.

When Kyle found out, there was hardly anything said about it. We went to the bank, and we were able to get a loan that would be enough money to get us out of the hole I had put us in. I was right; Kyle didn't even question me how this happened. Anyone else would have been furious, and would have had every right to be.

I was doing things that were out of character for me. I was irresponsible. I was not making good decisions. I went on as if nothing were wrong with me. I tried so hard to show everyone I was happy. I wasn't happy, though. Why was I unhappy? I had everything I ever wanted.

My mother had moved to another town a few years ago. We didn't keep in contact as much anymore. Debbie, my sister, and I talked often. Teresa had moved to Dallas, and I rarely saw her. I was very close to Debbie, but, still I didn't tell Debbie I wasn't happy anymore.

I didn't even tell my closest friends, Tracy and Delaine. They had been my friends since high school. I just couldn't tell them I wasn't happy.

Tracy and I had grown to be very close, and we had a great friendship. Tracy listened to me in a way that made me know she cared. We enjoyed being around each other, and had long conversations on the phone. We would visit each other and talk and talk. Tracy helped me a lot—more than she probably knew. She was a friend I could always confide in. I didn't know how to tell her I was unhappy. I had put on such a front. So, I held it all inside. The problem was I still didn't know exactly why I had become unhappy. I didn't know how to tell anyone I was unhappy, even I didn't know why I felt the way I did.

I couldn't tell anyone I was paranoid about people talking about me all the time. I didn't feel anyone liked me in our whole town. I didn't like that I was doing things I wouldn't normally do. I was spending money; I wanted to sleep all the time. I was never a morning person, and I always slept a lot, but now I wanted to lie in the bed or on the couch almost every day.

There was little conversation between Kyle and me, and we seemed to drift apart. We never discussed our feelings to each other. He worked, and I took care of the girls. I never did master being very affectionate to him. I wanted to do more things as a family. I felt something was missing in our marriage, and I wanted a closer relationship with my husband, but it didn't ever seem to happen. I didn't know how to make our marriage be the way I wanted it. I couldn't tell if Kyle was happy, either.

I met Mother for lunch one day, and told her I was leaving Kyle. I didn't have much explanation besides my unhappiness, and she didn't question me why. That's how Mother was, though. We still did not talk about personal things very much. Mother would ask me in general how I was doing, and I would always say, "fine." That was the extent of it, even if I wasn't doing well. No matter what was happening in our lives, Mother and I just didn't discuss personal things.

Our marriage was over. Kyle had gone out of town for a week to a training course for his job. The night he came back, I told him I was leaving. We didn't say much to each other. I didn't even give him much explanation as to why I was leaving. We went to bed and slept together that night. The next morning, I gathered my clothes, clothes for Tara and Kayla, and a few other things. My girls and I left and went to Mother's.

My perfect family had crumbled. A life that should have made me happy was all over. I left my husband of almost eight years. I left my friends and the small town I had lived in for ten years.

ON MY OWN

My mother had moved a few years back to another house she had bought. Teresa and her family had moved back from Dallas. They lived in the house Mother moved from, in Tyler. The house had a garage apartment that had been built for my grandmother, Nonnie. She didn't live there very long, though, before she went to a nursing home, so I moved into the garage apartment. That would be mine and Tara's and Kayla's home now. The apartment had a small living room and kitchen, one bedroom and a bathroom. It was small but it was perfect for us right then. Tara, Kayla, and I had our own place. The good thing about it was Teresa was right there, too.

I didn't know what I was to do now. My divorce was made final quickly. I was a single Mother now. I had to provide on my own now for my girls. I had to find a job. I had to bring home the money now. How could I do all that? I was scared and worried.

I got a job fairly quickly at a craft store. I didn't make much money there, so I quit that job. I found another job at a restaurant as a hostess. I didn't make much money there, either, and the hours I worked kept me away from Tara and Kayla more than I wanted. I quit that job, too. Debbie worked at a department store, and she told me to apply for a job there. Christmas was coming, and I was hired on as Christmas help. I still wasn't making enough money for us. I was working nights and weekends, just as I had at the other two jobs. I wanted to work at a job where I would have more time with Tara and Kayla. While I worked, Tara and Kayla stayed with a lady who had kept Debbie and Teresa's kids at one time.

I was so glad I lived closer to Debbie and Teresa now. I basically lived with Teresa and her family. There was a door that led from the garage apartment to the house. Most of the time at home, I stayed in the house with them instead of my garage apartment.

The girls and I ate supper in the evenings with Teresa and her family most of the time. If we weren't eating with Teresa, we would go to Debbie's and eat supper with her and her family. I was sad, again. Why had I left my husband? I was eating more and more as time passed, and I gained a lot of weight in just a short time. I gained up to three sizes bigger than my usual weight since I had left Kyle. I had been thin, but now I was getting bigger than I had ever been in my life. I hated it, but I kept on eating. Normally, when I was stressed out, I didn't have an appetite. This time, I couldn't seem to stop eating.

Depression was hovering over me again. I was just trying to cope with all the changes in my life now. I was finding it difficult to carry on from day to day. I didn't realize depression was taking over my life once again.

Teresa worked at a hospital, and she told me about a position they were hiring someone for. I applied for the job, and I was hired. This job meant that I would be working eight to five now. This would be so much better. I would be at home with Tara and Kayla every evening and on the weekends they weren't at their Daddy's.

Teresa and her family moved to another house not far from Mother's house, which they had been living in. I moved into a nice apartment on the other side of town. It was a good size for us, with two bedrooms, so I had my own room. Tara and Kayla had their own room now, and they had their own bed. They wouldn't have to sleep with me anymore. This would be good for my girls and me.

I went back to the house in Alba, where I had lived in with my family. The family I had with a daddy, a momma, and our two children. I went there to get some of the furniture and some kitchen things, and I stood in the kitchen going through the silverware. I was packing up half of it for myself and leaving half of it for Kyle. How strange.

I had asked Kyle for a thousand dollars so I could make a down payment on a car, since I didn't keep the vehicle that I had when Kyle and I were married. I couldn't afford to make the payments on it. That was all I wanted. The house should be his. It was where he had lived all his life. I didn't want him to give me half of what it was worth. I sure didn't want it to be sold. It just wasn't mine anymore, and that was how it should be. I would start anew in the town I had grown up in until I was fifteen years old. I couldn't stay in the town I had lived in for ten years. The town was too small for both Kyle and me. I wanted to go back to where I was raised.

I didn't want to go home to my apartment after work every evening, so I didn't. I continued to go to Debbie's or Teresa's as soon as I picked up the girls every day after work. We would eat supper with Teresa or Debbie every evening. Tara and Kayla would play outside with Teresa's daughter Kelly, and her son Kody, and her twins, Nicole and Cory. When we went to Debbie's, she and I would sit on her front steps in front of their house, and we would talk while Tara and Kayla played with Debbie's kids, Caire and Calyn. I didn't have much to say these days, though. Debbie did most of the talking. I would go home just in time to give the girls their bath. I always tucked them into bed and sometimes read one of their little books to them. That seemed to be all I could manage to do with them now.

I reached the point when I wasn't playing with Tara and Kayla, or reading to them much anymore. I just didn't have it in me to do those things like I had always done before with them. It was such an effort, but it shouldn't have been.

How could I go home to our apartment? How could Tara and Kayla enjoy being with me? I wasn't fun to be around. All I was thinking now was "poor me." How was I to go on this way? I needed to be around Debbie or Teresa. They were my safety net. Tara and Kayla would enjoy being at their house more than they would be just being with me. I wasn't giving what my girls needed from me as their momma. They needed much more attention from me than I was able to give.

I was imposing on my sisters' time with their families. That was all right though; I needed them. I was pathetic. When I was at Debbie's sitting on her front steps, I would just hang my head in my hands and wonder what was I going to do.

When I went to Teresa's, I would watch her cook while I sat at her kitchen table. I never helped her cook or clean up after we ate. I would talk more to Teresa than I did to Debbie about how I was feeling. I would sit and scratch my head and rub my face. I would tell Teresa how horrible my life was. I would tell her I should've stayed with Kyle. I would tell her I had everything there with him. I would say to her, "If I could only go back." She would tell me I had wanted to leave, and it would be the same as it was if I had stayed there. She would tell me everything would be all right, and that I was doing well. She was trying to convince me everything was going well for me. In my head, though, it was all bad for me now. I couldn't help the way I felt. I didn't want to hear I was doing well. I didn't want to hear I was able to make it on my own. I was not doing well. I did not want to do everything on my own. Couldn't Debbie and Teresa see what I was going through? I was in a terrible state.

I did have my own place. I had a new car. I was making pretty good money now. I received child support from Kyle. I had enough money to pay all my bills, and I made sure I paid all my bills on time. That was one thing I knew I had to do. There was no need for me to feel so down and sad. I didn't have to worry about money, but I did. I shouldn't really have any worries. I was very lonely now, though. What had I done? That question kept going over and over in my head.

Every evening after I complained to my sisters, I would go home to my apartment. I did my little routine of giving Tara and Kayla a bath. I would wash their hair every other night. I did always tuck them into bed. I did kiss them and tell them, "I love you." As for me, though, I didn't take a bath or a shower. I didn't take one in the mornings, either. I wasn't dirty. I just went to work and sat most all day. I put deodorant on every morning. I kept my underarms shaved. As long as I did that, it was all right that I didn't bathe. I wasn't washing my hair very often. No one would know I didn't bathe or didn't wash my hair. I couldn't put forth the effort.

Tara and Kayla were still such good girls. I rarely ever had to scold them. They must have wondered why we had left their daddy. They needed comfort from me. I was not being a good mother again. I didn't want Tara and Kayla to grow up with an unhappy momma. That was one reason I convinced myself to leave Kyle. Well, now their momma was even more unhappy. I felt guilt pour all over me because I took my girls away from their daddy.

Tara and Kayla would go to their daddy's every other weekend. There were times I would lie on the couch when they left, and I would lie there all weekend. I didn't want to do anything. I couldn't make myself do anything. When it was time for them to come home on Sunday, I would get up off the couch. I wouldn't call or go to Debbie or Teresa's to see them while the girls were gone. I could be alone when Tara and Kayla were gone. I didn't have to pretend their momma was all right.

I began to call Mother every morning when I got up to go to work. I hadn't been talking to Mother much for a while. Mother answered the phone every morning, and she would listen to me tell her I didn't know what I was going to do. I would sit there on the phone, smoking one cigarette after another. I had smoked since I was thirteen years old. Now, I smoked more than I ever had. I would listen to her as she told me to get dressed for work. She would tell me to get Tara and Kayla up and dressed. "You can do it," she would say. These are the things she told me every morning. This had gotten to be how I had to start my day. After she told me all those things, I would hang up the phone knowing I had to do it, and I would.

I would get up and get dressed, then I would get Tara and Kayla up and dressed, and leave. If they didn't eat breakfast before we left, I stopped at the corner store and got them breakfast on the way. I took them to the baby-sitter and went to work.

I never missed work. I knew I had to go to work. That is what you do. I was quiet and didn't talk much to people at work. I made sure I held myself together, and was able to do my job well. Everyone there was very nice, and I did like my job. My boss was a very kind man, and he was funny. He was easy to work for, and he made me feel appreciated. As long as I did my job, he was happy with me. We would sit and talk sometimes, and I began to talk to him a little about my personal life.

I was still sad and down. I made an appointment to go see a counselor at a local mental health facility. It was according to my income as to what I had to pay. It wasn't very expensive, which helped. I talked to my boss about going since I would have to take off work on the days that I had an appointment. He told me to do what I needed to do.

My first time there, I didn't care for the counselor I saw. I wasn't very comfortable talking to her. Actually, when I went to see her, the conversation seemed to always end up about her. I went a few times, but I didn't see that it was helping me, so I quit going.

Debbie suggested that I go see my psychiatrist. Debbie could always see the signs when I was depressed. Teresa agreed with Debbie about my going. I hadn't gone to see him in two years, and I didn't want to go. I didn't need medication again. I had not lost any weight, and I knew if I took the medication, it would make me gain weight like it had before. I would be fine. I didn't like my psychiatrist from the first time Mother and Debbie took me to his office. I knew I had to get over this, though. I called his office and made an appointment.

When I went to see him, he gave me a prescription. It was the same anti-depressant he had given me before, two years ago. I took the medication. I still didn't believe I needed it, but I did start feeling better. I stopped taking my medication after a few months, and I didn't go back to the psychiatrist.

I was going home after work, now. I was fixing supper for Tara and Kayla in the evenings. We would watch some TV, if we could see it on the snowy screen. I didn't have cable TV. No big deal, because by the time we got home and ate, it was almost time for the girls to take their baths and go to bed. I was giving Tara and Kayla more attention now. I had told myself I had to be better for them. My girls would not want a momma like me. I had to be happy, and then my girls would be happy. I wanted them to always be happy.

There was a girl, she was younger that I, that lived in my apartment complex who babysat for a lady a few doors down from me. We would talk as Tara and Kayla played with the little girl she babysat, and I enjoyed talking to her. I had fit someone else in my life other than my sisters and Mother.

On weekends when Tara and Kayla went to their daddy's, my new friend and I would go to a club. I danced and drank beer, and I was meeting some guys. I felt great now. I went from one extreme to another. I wasn't feeling sad anymore. I wanted to do things now. I was bathing. I was dressing nicely now. I felt good again. I had a lot of energy, and was talking a lot more now. Being a single mom was no problem now. My girls were my life again. I was a good mother again. I was happy again. I wanted to be around people now. I wasn't avoiding them anymore.

I was doing even a better job at work. I began to talk to my co-workers. I enjoyed going to work now. I was even voted employee of the month. I felt so much better. Just like that, I had gotten all better. It seemed as though one day I felt horribly depressed, and the next day I wasn't. I had been depressed for about six months, but it had left now.

I now wanted another man in my life. I wanted to be married again. When would I find someone? I wanted to marry soon. I had to have a husband. I didn't want to be alone. I feared I might be alone for the rest of my life.

Tara started her first year of school, and I took her to her first day and met her teacher. I was excited about Tara's starting school. She would love school, I knew, and she did. I loved to see the papers she brought home. She was learning so much. She loved to learn, just as she always had.

I took Tara and Kayla to their baby-sitter every morning. The baby-sitter took Tara to school, and Kayla would play with the other kids. When Tara was picked up from school, she would be back with Kayla.

Kayla had a personality that attracted people. She always had a smile on her face. Kayla was vocal. She would laugh and make other people laugh. She was a people person, who loved attention. I had the best girls in the whole world.

One day, I had a very slow day at work. I was so bored. I had done all my duties, and I wanted something to do. I would just leave for a little while. I left work and didn't tell anyone I was leaving. I went to the mall, and I was gone over an hour, maybe two. I worked in central supplies, and my boss wasn't there that day. All the supplies for the hospital were back in the area I worked. If something was needed for a patient, I was called to take it to where it needed to go. This meant that if a patient was in the emergency room and supplies were needed, I was to take them to the nurse. If we didn't have what was needed, I was to call one of the other hospitals in town and see if we could get it from them, and if so, I would go pick it up. This was part of my job. I didn't need to be leaving my job just because I was bored and wanted something to do.

On the way back to work, it hit me. I was thinking. "Why did I just leave work? That was crazy." I was scared to go back. What if someone knew I was gone? I didn't do things like that. I could be fired. What was I thinking? My job was important. I had to work. When a person has a job, he or she goes every day and does the very best job they can do. How irresponsible of me! When I got back to my job, no one knew I had ever left, thank God. I could never do that again. That was just wrong, very wrong.

Teresa had moved to North Carolina a few months ago. When they decided to move, I was devastated. How would I survive without her? How could I stay at my job without her there? I felt stronger now, though. It would be all right. I would miss her so much, but I would survive.

I wasn't going to Debbie's as much anymore. I wasn't calling Mother every morning. I was making it on my own without clinging to anyone. I was feeling good. I had confidence. I took Tara and Kayla grocery shopping. I took them out to eat. I read to them at bedtime. We laughed together again.

I had gotten past my depression, and I felt great. I was living my life once again. I wanted to go forward instead of backwards.

Second Time Around

I met a guy at work, Vick, who delivered supplies to the hospital, and he came to the hospital usually once a week. We would say a few things to each other and flirt sometimes. It felt nice to have a man who I thought took interest in me. I still desperately wanted to be married again.

He stopped coming to deliver supplies. I told the new guy that was delivering them now, to tell Vick to call me sometime. We began to talk on the phone often, almost daily. He lived in another state, a couple of hours away. He invited me to come and stay with him for a weekend. I had only known him a short time. Should I go? Was he someone that might be a weirdo? I had only seen him when he came to my job. But I didn't think carefully about any of those things. All that mattered was that I was having a relationship with someone.

I did decide to go to his house for a weekend, when the girls were at their daddy's, and I had a good time. He said all the right things to me and gave me the feeling that this could get serious. I desperately wanted to be married again.

I went to see him the next couple of weekends when Tara and Kayla went to their daddy's. I told Vick I wanted him to meet my girls. He came the next weekend to meet them. They were quiet around him. They were seeing momma with a different man other than their daddy. Kayla hid behind a chair. That was very unusual for her to be shy. It was normal for Tara to be standoffish when she first met someone. Neither Kayla nor Tara had much to do with him.

It was winter now. The year was 1988, and I was twenty-six years old. Tara was six years old, and Kayla was four. I had been divorced a little over a year. I had spent half of the year being sad and depressed. The next half of the year, I began to rocket to an unusual energy level.

I continued to see Vick. We talked on the phone every day, and most every night, and we saw each other on the weekends. We had moved so fast in a very short time.

Vick and I went to a club one night, and when we left, we went to eat breakfast at a restaurant next door. He had been drinking, and so had I. While we were there eating, he popped the question. He asked me to marry him. Of course, I told him yes. I would marry again. I would not be alone. The thought never crossed my mind that I had only known him a couple of months. I was going to be married, and that's all that mattered to me. This would be the second time around for me as a bride.

I moved in with Vick, and I left the state I thought I would never leave. I left my job. This was ridiculous. I was stupid. I really didn't really even know this man. What kind of person was he? Would I be happy with him? I didn't think of any of that. I was impulsive. This is exactly what I wanted, to have a husband again. I was so happy, or so I thought.

My sex drive had become huge. Sex was almost all I wanted to do with Vick. Every night when we went to bed, it was hours of sex. When we were alone, I wanted it. Every chance we had, that's what we did. I thrived on it.

I married Vick four months after we met. We had gone to a jewelry store to get our rings, and I picked out the ones I wanted. I traded the wedding rings I had from my previous marriage, and I paid for the remainder of the cost of the new ones. It was a stupid thing to do, sell my rings Kyle had given me, and buy my own wedding rings. Ding, ding—the man was to buy my rings. Why did I do that? It didn't matter. I hardly gave it a thought. I was not thinking clearly. This was all happening on a whim. I didn't really think any of it out clearly. I just did it.

Shortly after we were married, Vick's eighteen month old daughter, Brittney, from his previous marriage, came to live with us. His ex-wife's son, Lott, from her previous marriage came to live with us, also. Lott was four years old, Tara was six, and Kayla was four now. We were a family of six now. I welcomed Brittney and Lott when they came to live with us. I had four children now.

Vick went to work every morning. He drove my car to work because his vehicle didn't run. I was a housewife again. Tara started her new school. Kayla, Lott, and Brittney stayed home every day with me.

When Tara came home from school they would all play together and they played well together. They all got along. When it was time for Vick to come home, I would cook supper. After we all ate, the kids got their baths, and shortly after that it was time for them to go to bed. The girls shared a room, and Lott had his own room. Our kitchen and living room were in the middle of the trailer. Vick's bedroom and mine was at the opposite end from the kids' rooms.

Kyle did not like the fact that I had moved to Shreveport, Louisiana, and taken the girls. He didn't like having to drive farther to pick them up. He was angry with me, and I knew he was. We had argued about it. I feared that he would pick them up and wouldn't bring them back. In reality, he would never do that.

Vick and I decided to try to get custody of Brittney and Lott. We were going through a custody battle, and Kyle was angry with me because I had moved. I was sure that I was going to lose all the kids. I felt sure Kyle was going to take Tara and Kayla, and I may not see them again. With the custody battle going on, I was afraid that Brittney and Lott would be taken away, too. My fears, at the time, were centered on the kids.

I became fearful my kids were going to be taken away from me. I began to think anyone might take them away from me. My mind was beginning to be consumed again by my fears. I had been so fearful of taking care of Kayla when she was born. I was now having fears attack me again. I didn't withdraw myself from the kids, as I had done with Kayla. I was determined to protect them from everybody.

I was not sleeping at night very much now. I couldn't sleep; I didn't want to sleep. I didn't feel like I needed to sleep. I tossed and turned every night in bed. Bad dreams came when I did fall asleep. I would dream of Daddy. Those dreams weren't bad, but the others were. I didn't always remember my dreams, but I would wake up from them being scared.

It was summer time, and I took the kids to the swimming pool in the trailer park we lived in during the day. I would lock my keys in the house, and we would be locked out. I did this at least three times in a matter of a few weeks. I was becoming forgetful.

When I left the house to go somewhere, I would forget how to get where I was going. I panicked when I locked us out of the house. I panicked when I got lost while I was driving.

When I went to the grocery store, I would forget what I was there to buy. I would walk around the store upset at myself because I couldn't remember what to get. I would look around to see if anybody might be able to tell I didn't know what to buy. I thought everyone was looking at me. I'd get to the checkout line and would get so anxious, I felt I had to get out of the store right away. I usually bought a box of tampons so no one would see me walking out without anything. I don't know why I bought tampons, maybe it was because I knew I had to have them eventually. The grocery store was close to the house. I would concentrate really hard on how to get there and back home, so I wouldn't get lost.

I didn't have any friends here. I was away from my family. Teresa still lived in North Carolina. I didn't call Mother, or Debbie, or anyone else because I didn't have a phone. I didn't go to see Mother or Debbie, and they didn't come to see me either. I hadn't talked to my friend Tracy in a long time. I missed her, and thought of her often. I didn't have my family, or friends here to talk to.

Vick and I went to his parents' house quite often, though. They were good people, and I did enjoy talking to them.

My mind was suspicious of people. I had strange thoughts all the time now. Vick didn't realize anything was different about me. After all, he really didn't know me. Even I didn't see what was happening to me. I was worried and scared mostly at night. I was afraid someone would come to the house and take my children. I was fearful of that every day now.

I stayed up almost every night. I carried myself through my days well, so I thought. I was never tired. I would go all day and all night without sleep.

I stayed up at night listening to the radio. It wasn't music I normally listened to. My music had always been mostly country, but the music I listened to at night now was more like rock or heavy metal. It was really weird music. While I listened to it I would look out the window often to see if anyone was coming up to our trailer house. I would sometimes move around in our living room swaying to the beat of the music while Vick and the kids slept. It didn't seem that Vick ever noticed that I was up all night.

One day I went to the store down the road from us. I used the pay phone, and I called Tracy and talked to her for awhile. Then I called Delaine and talked to her for a while, too. I talked like everything was great. I thought it was. They didn't know the state of mind I was in. We planned to meet in Tyler, Texas, at the mall. We decided on the day and time, and I went to the mall that day to meet them. We were to meet at the water fountain in the mall, but when I got there I didn't see them. I couldn't believe they weren't there. They knew I was coming to meet them. How could they forget? I had been so excited to see them. Now I was getting angry because they had stood me up. I walked up and down the mall, Tara and Kayla walking beside me.

I was getting suspicious that something was going to happen. I was thinking Tara and Kayla's uncle was going to come and take them. Every time I went somewhere with my girls, I thought they were going to be snatched away from me. I didn't know why I thought their uncle was going to come take them from me. I hadn't even thought of him in a long time, and he was a super nice guy. How could I ever think he would do that? I was anxious and nervous, and I was holding on to Tara and Kayla's hands very tightly. I was looking over my shoulder.

I finally decided to leave before he found me. I was even more anxious and nervous. I held on to Tara and Kayla's hands even more tightly as we walked through the mall. I was still looking over my shoulder. I got Tara and Kayla in the car and went home. I wasn't going to stay any longer, waiting to see Tracy and Delaine.

The next time I talked to Tracy, I asked her what happened to her and Delaine. I told her I couldn't find them. She said they were there, and that they couldn't find me. I told her about Tara and Kayla's uncle coming to take them away from me. She thought that was so strange, but she believed me, even though it wasn't true. My mind was suspicious of almost everyone. I never stopped being afraid that somebody was going to take my kids. I didn't talk to Tracy, or see her again until a few months later.

We lived close to an airport. When I lay in the bed at night, I would hear the airplanes fly over us. I thought they were watching us. They were watching my children, too. They would see that they were there. They would come in the morning and take them, I just knew it. I never heard the planes during the day.

Vick and I were still having sex most every night. I hadn't lost my desire for sex. I still wanted it all the time. After we had sex, I would talk to Vick for what seemed like hours. After I had talked so long, he would fall asleep. When he went to sleep is when I would go in the living room to listen to my music and look out the window next to our front door.

I knew in my head that someone was planning to come in and take my children. I started going and sitting in the girls' room at night to watch them sleep. I was not going to let anyone get to my children. I wasn't worried so much that Tara and Kayla's dad would come to get them. He wouldn't do that at night anyway. I was worried a stranger would come in and get them. Somebody, anybody, might come in and take them from me.

We were still going through the custody battle. I bought a notebook and began to write down when Brittney and Lott's mother came to get them, and when she brought them back. She didn't ever say much at all to me, nor did I say much to her.

Lott would sometimes cry at night and ask for his momma. I would try to comfort him by telling him it was all right. I would tell him his momma would come to see him again. I was feeling sad for Brittney and Lott's mother. I knew she loved them. She didn't come often to get them, and she would bring them back after a short time, but she still came to see them. I thought how awful it must have been for her not having them with her. I had stopped thinking she didn't want them, like I had at the beginning of all this. I didn't know her; I didn't know why she couldn't have her kids with her. I thought maybe something could be going on in her life and that she needed time to sort things out. Vick had told me, shortly before I moved in with him, that Brittney and Lott's momma had taken them to his parents' to stay with them. I didn't know why their momma had taken them to stay with Vick's parents.

The night before we were to go to court to find out if we would get custody of Brittney and Lott, we stayed at Vick's parents' house. His parents, his grandmother, and Vick's aunt all lived on a private road. They were the only ones that lived on that road, and their houses were close to each other.

That night I was up all night. I walked back and forth from the three houses. I walked from Vick's parent's house to his grandmother's house, and knocked on her door. I don't know what time of morning it was. Then I walked to Vick's aunt's house and knocked on her door. I went inside her house. I needed to go to sleep, but I couldn't. She and I talked for a little while. Afterwards, I walked back to Vick's parents. I walked up and down the road all night long. I could not lie down and go to sleep; my mind raced with all sorts of thoughts. I was anxious and very nervous about going to court that morning. My mind was foggy. I felt like I was just dragging myself as I walked up and down that road. When morning came, I didn't know if I had dreamed walking the road all night, or if I had actually done that.

Vick and I, and his parents went to the courthouse that morning. When we got to the courthouse, we went inside and stood outside of the courtroom we would go into. We were to go in one at a time. I watched all the people around me in the courthouse, but I still felt I was in a fog.

I saw a man just down the hallway from us. It was a man I had met at a club one night about four or five months after Kyle and I were divorced. I had gone to his house one night. Maybe it was someone else's house; I'm not sure. Lots of people were there. The house was very nice and secluded. All the furnishings were extravagant. After I got there, another man went and looked all inside my car. I wondered why he was looking in my car. Did he think something was there? What would be in my car he could be interested in? I was thinking all the people were doing drugs. Why did I come here? I didn't know this guy well at all. I had only known him for a few weeks. Everyone was well dressed, and they all looked to be wealthy. I thought they must be drug trafficking. Everyone in the house was mingling and talking and drinking wine and mixed drinks. I didn't feel comfortable there at all. I had smoked weed before, but I had always been scared of doing more serious drugs. I thought if I did any drugs, I would be that person that died the first time I tried them. I had never gotten involved with street drugs or people who used drugs.

What was I to do now? I was scared to leave. I was scared to stay. The house was huge and spacious. The man I had met at the club and I went into a bedroom and stood and talked there for a short while. I don't know what the conversation was about. I had been there maybe an hour, and I was ready to leave. I told him I had to go. When I did leave, I was relieved to be away from there. I was still wondering why that man looked in my car. Did they think I was a cop? Did they think I would tell what was going on there? Actually, I didn't see any drugs or anything else suspicious there. I just had an eerie feeling about it all. It scared me after I left. If they did have drugs there, would they suspect that I might tell someone what I thought they were doing. I never wanted to see that guy again.

When I saw the man I had gone to that house to see that one night, I wondered why he was at this courthouse. It frightened me. He was wearing a black leather jacket. He looked as if he had plenty of money, like all the other people at that house had that night. He was part of the mafia. It had all come together in my mind. They were dealing drugs at that house. They all looked wealthy, and they were all part of the mafia. That is why the guy had searched inside my car. I was sure of it. I didn't want him to see me. I would never tell anyone that this man was mafia, never. I was afraid to.

If I were in my right mind, I would never have thought that. Those kinds of thoughts would never have entered my mind. This man at the courthouse was not the same man I had met several months ago. No one could convince me otherwise, though. My mind was really playing tricks on me, but I didn't realize it. It was all so real to me.

Vick, his family, and I were still waiting for our case to begin. If I had truly acted so weird last night, Vick and his parents' must have been wondering what I would say when I was called to the witness stand. I was being very quiet, and still watching everyone in the hallway. I felt strange, as if I were in a dream, but I knew I wasn't. I think Vick and his parents were worried I'd blow the whole case. I wasn't thinking about what questions I would be asked or what I would say.

My name was called to go in the courtroom. I walked up to the witness stand at the front of the courtroom and was asked, "Do you swear to tell the whole truth and nothing but the truth?"

I said, "I do."

My mind was still foggy; almost blank. They were finished with me now. I didn't know what they had asked me, or what I had told them.

I went back out into the hallway, and we waited for a little while. Then someone said, "We won."

It was all over. We had Brittney, but Lott had to go back to his momma's because he wasn't Vick's biological son.

My thoughts and fears became worse. I was still sure someone was going to come and take my children away from me. I was much more paranoid now. I felt that everyone around me was watching me everywhere I went.

If I saw a police car and the kids were in my car, I panicked. They were looking for me. I just knew it. I would keep my eye on the police car until it was out of sight. Kyle, my ex-husband had told them where to find me. If they spotted me, they would follow us to our house. The police would get Tara, and Kayla, and Brittney. I would be terrified. I wanted to hurry and get home so all my kids would be safe. These were my thoughts.

One night, Vick left the house to go to the store. I heard someone outside, and I didn't have any idea that it was Vick. I didn't even think it might be him. I picked up a shotgun we had in our house. Who was coming in my house? I knew it was someone to get my children. I would not let them take my children. I would do anything to make sure of that. I had become fearful that someone was going to get them and take them away from me shortly after I moved in with Vick. I began to have all these fears when the custody battle started with Vick's ex-wife. I knew Kyle was angry with me for moving, and I feared he would take Tara and Kayla away from me. When they stayed a weekend with him, I always wondered if he would bring them back. I stayed suspicious of almost everybody.

Vick opened the front door. He barely got in the house when I raised the shotgun at him. He stayed very calm and took the gun from me. I didn't know if he was scared or what he thought, and I didn't really think about that. I don't know what happened after he took the gun from me. In my state of mind, who knows if I could have shot him. I didn't realize I had done that until much later.

I was sitting in my living room one night and I got my pen and paper. Vick and the kids were in bed. I didn't write about how I was feeling as I had when I was a teenager. I began to write letters. I wrote to Teresa in North Carolina. I wrote to my friend Tracy. I was thinking of whom I should write. I had to write and tell them how much I loved them, and I had to let them know how very special they were to me. Something might happen to me, and they would not know how I felt about them. I thought I might die, or I would go away. I might not ever see them again. I was very homesick. Everyone who had meant so much to me seemed terribly far away. My letters had to be sent to them soon before something happened to me. I wasn't suicidal; I just had a feeling that I might never see any of them again.

Vick had figured out that something was wrong with me. He didn't really know what, but something was definitely wrong. He called Mother one day and told her I was not well. She told him we were just having marital problems, and that everything would be all right. He told her that we never argued, and we weren't having any marital problems. We didn't ever argue. He couldn't make her believe that something was really wrong with me.

Vick called her again on another day. This time he convinced her I was not well. Mother came to our house to get me, and she gathered some of my clothes to take. She went in our bedroom where there were several Playboy magazines. She seemed furious, and, with a stern voice, she said, "This is what's wrong with her."

Normally, I would have been totally embarrassed, but I wasn't. I didn't think anything about the magazines that were under the bed, although having that type of magazines was not something I would normally have in my home.

Mother and I got in Mother's car. Sadness fell all over me. I was leaving here. Where were we going? I didn't know what was going on. I didn't understand why Mother had come to get me. I felt as if I were in a daze, and I couldn't figure out why Mother was taking me with her. Tara and Kayla stayed with Vick.

All this time, I didn't think anything was wrong with me. I was actually living in my own world with the horrific thoughts in my head. Nobody knew what I was thinking. My family didn't even know I was having these strange and bizarre thoughts. I never talked about them or told anyone I was fearful that someone was going to take my children away. I believed all my thoughts were real. They were to me. I was living outside of reality.

I was completely quiet on the way to Mother's house. Mother wasn't saying anything, either. I looked out the window, watching the cars and everything we passed. I'm sure Mother told me we were going to her house, but what was going on wasn't really sinking in. When we got to her house, I got out of the car and went inside the house.

One day, after being at Mother's a few days, I went into a corner in Mother's house and curled up holding my knees up to my face and began to rock. What was wrong with me? Something had to be done. Mother and Debbie talked, and they knew they had to do something to find out what was wrong with me. The next thing I knew, Mother, Debbie, and I were in the car going somewhere. We drove up to University Park Hospital in Tyler, Texas. We walked in the front door and passed a very large fish tank. I thought it was pretty, with the fish and other colorful things in it. I just followed Mother and Debbie through the hospital. I couldn't figure out why we were there.

I had not taken any medication for my depression since I had lived in my apartment eight months ago. I didn't need it, so I didn't continue taking what my doctor had prescribed me. I didn't think it made any difference if I took it or not. I had gotten better and was enjoying life. I was carefree and ready for excitement, so why should I have kept taking the anti-depressant? I had gone from depression to an unnatural high.

Behind Locked Doors

When Mother, Debbie, and I went inside the hospital, we were led to a nurse's station. I was checking myself into this hospital. It was a rehabilitation/behavioral hospital. I was given papers to fill out, and I was coherent filling out all the papers they gave me. They asked my name and what the day and date were. I knew all the answers. After I filled out the papers they had given me, Mother and Debbie left. What was going to happen now?

I was taken to a room in which I placed my clothes. There were patient's rooms one by one down a hall. I checked myself in the unit where we were led to, which was the family room in this unit. There were round tables with chairs set up in this room. There was a piano and dominoes. There were pieces of cardboard covered with felt that had pictures on them. There were markers to color the pictures. There was a long bar with nurses sitting behind it.

There was another room off to the right from the family room, with a TV in it, and folding chairs lined up in rows facing the TV. I would eventually find that there was another room at the end of the nurse's station.

There was a door on one side of the family room that led to a very small place outside with a patio table. This area had a tall privacy fence that surrounded it. At the opposite end of the family room was another small place outside. There was a patio table there, also, and there was a tall privacy fence around that area, too. No one could see beyond the privacy fence.

When I checked myself in, I was told the same thing as I was when I was admitted into the psyche ward after I had Kayla. They told Mother, Debbie, and me, they would keep me here for two weeks. After two weeks, they would see how I was doing. What was up with being told they would keep me here for two weeks? Mother and Debbie had been told two weeks is how long they would keep me in that psyche ward five years ago. Being told two weeks there and now two weeks here stuck with me. Two weeks, two weeks.

I was given medication right away, just as they had done in the psyche ward before, but I was given even more here. They would monitor my medication here. It seemed every day another pill was added to my little paper cup. I hated taking the pills. My pills were all different colors: pink, white, blue and others.

A nurse would call me up to the bar, the nurse's station.

"Here's your medication, Melody," the nurse would say.

Yeah, great, and what are these pills going to do for me? My pills were all different shapes. They were round, octagonal, and oval. There was one that had, I believe, a star shape cut out of the middle of it.

I would pour my pills out of my little cup on to the nurses' bar, to me the nurses' station was similar to a bar in a restaurant, or a club. I would look at my pills and play with them. I would sometimes put them in a circle or lay the octagon on one of its sides. It would sit there all by itself. It wouldn't fall over unless I slightly hit it. I would delicately twirl the round one with my finger. I named some of my pills.

One pill was Haldol. I named it "hello doll." One was Moban, and I called it "no man." I was fascinated with the shapes, colors, and names they were called. What a joke. It was like candy; candy I hated.

The nurse would say, "Melody, just take your medication." Reluctantly, I'd be a nice girl, and put them back in my little cup. I poured them in my mouth and swallowed them down with water from my small clear plastic cup. At times, the nurse would carry her tray around taking it to one person to another one, handing each person his or her little paper cup. I hated it when I was given my pills to take. I would have loved to knock her tray out of her hands and have the water fly up in her face, but I didn't. I would pour the pills in my mouth and chase them down with the water from my small clear plastic cup every time. Soon, my little white cup had several pills in it. There were five, six, seven; two or three times a day at least. How many pills, how many times a day?

The first days I was there I just observed everyone. One girl walked like a zombie. One girl walked around singing and snapping her fingers. Some people were old, some were young, and some were in-between.

How sad this place was. It was scary. Everyone was a stranger to me. This place was full of crazy people. I guess I fit right in. I was crazy, too.

Mother and Debbie would come to see me. I wasn't happy to see them. I was just numb to everything that was happening to me. I could see Mother was smiling, though I knew it was difficult for her. I would sit down at a table, and Mother would sit down beside me. I would get up and go to another table. Then she would come and sit by me again. I was so aggravated at her. Don't bother me, Mother. Just leave me alone. This is what I wanted to say to her, but I didn't. I didn't know why I felt this way towards Mother.

Mother's face showed sorrow and sadness sometimes. She didn't know what to do. She didn't know what to say. I could see that she ached inside with pain. She couldn't hide it from me. She tried so desperately to let me know everything would be all right. She tried to hide her fears of not knowing what was wrong with me. I had never seen fear in Mother's eyes, ever, but it was there now. I could see it when I looked at her. I saw through all her smiles and the sweet, kind words she said to me. I did not want her around me.

I could no longer believe the words Mother had always told me anymore. "It's going to be all right," are the words she would say. It didn't matter what was going on in my life or hers. It would just simply be all right. This time, where I was and how I was, wasn't all right.

Debbie would come with her make-up on, her lipstick, and her nice clothes. Her hair was always fixed, and she was so pretty. I looked awful, just pathetic; but she was always pretty. Why couldn't I be pretty? I was in a horrible place, but she was free. She came here and she left here. I had to stay. I was locked up. When could I leave this place? Would I leave this place?

Teresa had moved back from North Carolina after I had been in the hospital for a short time. She, Mother, and Debbie had been communicating over the phone before she moved back. Teresa could not grasp what I was going through. She had searched for reading material, books, and any other kind of information about mental illness, but there was very little to be found. She moved back to Tyler so she could be near me. She did not want to be that far away from her sister, not knowing what would happen to me. I never saw Teresa at the hospital. When she did come, I wasn't aware of it.

I began to play dominoes with the old men that were there. They were so sweet. Why were they here? It was strange to see these old men there. They would always sit at a table and talk and play dominoes, so I had joined them. As we played dominoes, they talked to me. I didn't say much to them, though. I would just listen. I loved to play forty-two. I remembered playing it with my friends when I lived in Alba, and now I was playing with old men I didn't know.

The old men were the only people in there I really cared to sit with and talk to. I didn't want to talk to anyone else. I didn't know what to say to other people there. The old men would tell me stories about when they were young and the things they had done in their lives. I loved listening to them. For some reason, I found comfort in them.

I would sit at a table and color the felt pictures with the markers. I got so sick of coloring felt. At first it was calming. I would focus on my coloring, trying to get it just perfect. I would pick out the perfect colors for everything in the pictures.

After a while, I didn't want to color the fuzzy felt anymore. It had become very boring and monotonous.

There was nothing to do here. I wasn't playing dominoes much anymore. I wasn't sitting with the old men as often. I didn't color any more. I hated sitting in the family room watching everyone here. It was the same old thing, day after day.

What day was it? I didn't know. I didn't care what time it was or what day it was. I didn't even think about it. Why should I care what time it was? I wasn't going anywhere. There was not anything worth watching the time for. It was all bad here, all day long. There wasn't any time of the day that I looked forward to.

Someone new would check in here, and when the new person arrived, he or she would sometimes ask me how long I had been here. My answer was always the same; I would tell them two weeks and then walk away from them. I did not want to have conversations with anyone. I was told I'd be here two weeks. I got stuck at two weeks. I had no concept of time.

My friends that I went to high school with, Tracy and Delaine, came to see me one day. I was thrilled to see them. They sat with me and talked to me in the family room. I was not the same person they knew. I was different before all this happened to me. I had been normal, but now I was out of my mind. They made me laugh, and I made them laugh. I thought, "They think I'm funny and crazy." I guess I was funny and very crazy. The laughter did wonders for me. I would get up from the table where we were sitting, and then I would sit back down with them. It was hard for me to sit still.

Tracy would say, "Just sit back down, Melody."

I didn't know what was wrong with me. I don't think Tracy and Delaine did, either. They gave me hope by acting like nothing at all was wrong with me. It didn't matter to them that I was up and down or wondering around the family room. Even though I was crazy, Tracy and Delaine loved me. I was their friend and they were mine, no matter what. It was like old times when we used to sit at our kitchen tables and talk for hours.

This place was so depressing. My nights were still the very worst part of my days. I could not sleep. I went day after day without sleep. Night after night, I did not sleep.

At night when I would walk out of my room and go down the hall, I would only get to the middle of the hall.

"Melody, go back to your room," the nurse called out loudly to me.

I just wanted to go to the family room. There were lights on in that room. There was noise. The nurses were talking and sometimes laughing. Why couldn't I be in the family room? I wanted to be in that room, not my room. I would attempt to walk down the hall again.

The nurse would again say loudly, "Melody, go back to your room."

My room was dark. I would try to lie down. I couldn't be still; I would toss and turn. Get up, lie down, get up, and lie down, over and over. There were all kinds of weird thoughts in my head. I couldn't stop them. My mind just raced and raced. I would pace the floor in my room. Let daylight come, please. The weird thoughts in my head stopped when morning came.

I would hear this same noise night after night. It was Mother outside my window. Her husband was out there, too. I could hear horses running. I could hear them telling the horses to getty-up. I could hear a whip whipping someone. Mother was whipping my husband, Vick. He was crawling on the ground. It was a clear picture in my head.

Mother would shout to him, "Go on, and get out of here. Get out of here."

Why were they outside my window? I didn't understand why Mother was whipping Vick and yelling at him to go on. Mother's husband had horses he kept in a pasture near where they lived. These were the horses they were riding.

There was something else that happened often at night. Mother would be in the family room. I could hear her shouting. She was standing on a platform. There was a line of men in front of her. I didn't know any of the men. Mother had a bullwhip. She would whip one man at a time. She would whip one, and then another man would step up to the platform. She whipped all of them one by one. She was shouting at them. I couldn't make out what she was saying. What had these men done? Mothers' voice was full of anger. I would lie in my bed in my room at night and hear her. I would walk out of my room to go to the family room where they were. I could hardly get past my door before a nurse would tell me to go back to my room. This picture in my mind was real. It was just as real as the picture outside my window when Mother and her husband would come on their horses. Vick was always there crawling on the ground. This is what happened at night when I was supposed to be sleeping.

I was not eating now. I was given nutritional drinks. I wouldn't eat, so I had to drink the chocolate and vanilla drinks out of cans. I didn't like the vanilla, and I wouldn't drink that kind if they brought it to me. I would get mad if they brought me vanilla, so they started bringing me chocolate ones only.

We could smoke in the family room. People there would go up to the bar and ask a nurse for one of their cigarettes. I wanted a cigarette. I needed one badly. I would ask someone if I could have one of theirs'. People who smoked there would share their cigarettes with me.

Mother would ask me when she came to see me what she could bring me to eat.

"I'll bring you some pinto beans, stewed potatoes, and cornbread," she said with a look like she knew I would eat that. It was my favorite meal growing up. That was a meal I would eat until I was so full I felt like I would pop. Everyone was trying so hard to get me to eat.

One day when Mother asked if there was something she could bring me, I said, "Cigarettes!" just waiting for her to say she would. Of course, she would. Mother would get me anything, if she knew it would make me feel better.

Mother never knew I smoked. I had smoked for over twelve years, but I had hid it from her. I could never smoke in front of her because it would have been very disrespectful of me. I didn't think about how Mother would feel knowing I smoked. I desperately wanted my own cigarettes here. Mother didn't care that I wanted cigarettes. I had not told Mother to bring me anything until that day. I never wanted her to bring me anything. When she asked me that day, I needed cigarettes so badly. That was the only thing at the time I wanted from the outside world, other than to see it.

What I longed for was just to go outside. I would sit outside at one of patio tables every once in a while. Someone always had to go out there with me, usually someone who worked here. The doors that led outside to the patio tables were always locked. I wondered if they thought I might climb the fence and escape. When Mother, or Debbie came I was able to go and sit outside with them. Those were the only times I would get to go outside. I was locked up inside this place.

The privacy fence where the patio tables were was very tall. I couldn't see over it. I couldn't see through the boards that were nailed tightly side by side. Being outside felt fresh and gave me a small feeling of freedom. The sunlight and the sky with all the different shapes of clouds was the most wonderful scene at this place. The doors to the patio were locked as soon as I stepped out. When I had to come back in from my slight freedom, the door was locked as soon as I stepped inside. I was back in the most sad, depressing, horrible place I could ever be in. I was in a prison of craziness, true craziness.

I had to have someone watch me do everything and anything. The only thing I could do by myself was go to the bathroom. The only time I wasn't watched was when I was in my room at night. They sure did watch to make sure I didn't come out of my room, though.

I still was not eating. I told Debbie why I wouldn't eat. I don't know what the reason was, but it was a very real and serious thing to me. I lost weight and I lost more weight. My one hundred thirty-pound body had dwindled away to eighty-something pounds. There was no one who could convince me to eat. I was not going to eat.

Tara and Kayla came to see me one day. Their grandparents came and brought my girls with them. I was sitting in a chair, and Tara and Kayla's grandparents sat down beside me. I believe Mother and Debbie were there, too. They were all talking, but I didn't pay attention to what they were talking about. Tara and Kayla were playing around us. I wondered if they should sit down. Why weren't any of them making the girls sit down? They continued talking amongst themselves. I felt like they were ignoring me. Hadn't they come to see me? I was just watching them. I wasn't talking to them, and I wasn't talking to Tara and Kayla either. It was strange that they were here. What were my little girls thinking of me? I do not know how long they stayed and visited with me that day, but they never came again.

After I had admitted myself in the rahabilitation/behavioral health center, Tara and Kayla stayed with Vick. Then after a little time, they went to live with Mother.

I was kept in this place for much longer than everyone thought I would be. Tara and Kayla's dad eventually went to court to get custody of them. Mother was made power of attorney over me. She went to court in my behalf. The court's decision was to let Tara and Kayla stay with Mother, even though I was in the hospital because of a mental crisis. My girls were to stay with Mother until I was checked out of the hospital. I wasn't aware that all this had happened.

Tara and Kayla did go to live with their daddy after all. They needed their daddy, and he wanted them with him. He loved his girls.

My girls were so young: Tara was seven now, and Kayla was five. What were their thoughts through all of this? My girls were suffering; I know they must have.

I became sick with a very bad kidney infection. I would urinate on the floor, and I wasn't embarrassed when I did. Normally, I would have been. It was no big deal to me. I had no idea I had this serious infection.

Tracy, my friend who meant the world to me, continued faithfully coming to see me. While she was visiting me one day, I urinated on the floor.

"Melody, go to the bathroom," Tracy said, trying to hold back a laugh.

She wasn't laughing at me. She had made me laugh so hard I couldn't stop peeing. It felt great to laugh. There wasn't anything here to laugh about. Tracy had done a wonderful thing for me. She had made the sound of laughter come out of me, just as her and Delaine had done the day they came together. It was always great to see Tracy's face. She would hug me and smile at me and laugh with me.

Tracy had been there for me as a friend time and time again. Now she was there at the worst time of my life. She knew I was not the person she had known for nine years. She would not give up on the hope that I would get better. As always, when I saw her she totally brightened my day. But, when she would leave it would break my heart.

I began to bleed one day. Why was I bleeding? I was menstruating and didn't know it. It frightened me at first. I finally realized that the reason I was bleeding was because I had gotten my period.

But, then I thought, I was probably pregnant, and that I was having a miscarriage. Was I pregnant? I hadn't been taking any birth control. Did I lose my baby, or did these people here do something to kill my baby? They didn't want me to have a baby. All my thoughts were bizarre, but they were real to me.

One day, I wanted to take a shower. I don't know how often I took a shower, but I didn't remember taking a shower since I had come here. This day, I wanted to take a shower, though. I went up to the nurse's bar. I asked a nurse for a razor.

"Oh, no," the nurse said to me, as if I would use the razor for something more than just shaving under my arms.

"I want to shave my underarms," I said with anger, "that's all!"

I could read her face. She thought I would try to cut my wrist or do something along those lines. I don't know if I actually took a shower and used the razor or not. I don't know if she ever gave me a razor to use.

It seemed as though I was beginning to feel as if I were more in reality than I was at the beginning of my stay in here. I wanted out of this place. I was done with walking and sitting around so calmly, and talking so little. I was going to fight now. I became full of anger. I would show all these people here that I was definitely crazy. I began acting out with rage.

I had a tall, brown, wood closet in my room. It looked like a school locker, but it was much taller, probably about six feet tall. It was crammed full of clothes. I had the clothes I had brought with me when I checked myself in here. As I lost weight, Mother brought me more clothes. I had all kinds of clothes in my tall locker closet. Big clothes and small clothes, sweat pants, sweat shirts, jeans, tee-shirts.

I began to change my clothes constantly. I put my clothes on for the day. I would then go back to my room and put more clothes on over the ones I already had on. I would take clothes off and put different ones on. I would layer my clothes, layer after layer. Then I would go back and take them off and put different clothes on again. I would take them off and on, off and on, changing my clothes over and over. My clothes were strewn all over my room.

I could tell it was very annoying to the nurses and everyone else that worked here. I was aggravating all of them. One day I went to open my closet, and it was locked. Who locked my door? Every door in this place was locked.

It was the middle of the night, and I was furious that I couldn't get in my closet. I started banging it. I was determined to have access to my clothes. I pulled at the bottom of the closet door. I tried to pry it open any way I could. I hit it hard right above the handle on it, and lo and behold, it opened. Yes! I was back in my closet full of clothes. I had outsmarted them all.

I told one of the nurses one day I wanted to check myself out of this place.

"You have to talk to your doctor about that," she said to me.

"Where's my doctor?" I asked.

She told me he would be here at a certain time, like one o'clock. Time meant nothing to me. I didn't know what time it was, or when it would be one o'clock. I never asked what time it was. I never saw a clock in this place, if there was one. It was as if I couldn't even tell time.

Every time I asked the nurses about something, their reply was always, "You have to ask your doctor," or "No," or "You'll have to wait."

Almost everything I asked to do wasn't permitted. I wasn't allowed to do anything. I was bored. When would I be able to do something besides just sit in this place?

The amount of medication I took became ridiculous. More pills, different shapes and different colors. They would have to give me two little clear plastic cups, soon. My little cup was getting more and more full. I began to ask about my medication.

"What is this one? What does this pill do, or this one? Why do I take this one, and how does this pill help me?" I asked the nurses.

Once again their answer was, "You have to talk to your doctor about that."

Where the hell was my doctor? I rarely ever saw the huge man I didn't like. When I did see him, I didn't have enough time to ask him all my questions, or I forgot them. There were too many to remember.

There was a small room down a hall close to the nurse's bar. This room was the doctor's and my chat room. I would walk in the small room where I went to talk to him. He would say, "Come on in and sit down," in his deep voice.

I would follow him in the small room, and he would always go straight to a big, leather chair by a small window to the left of his chair. I sat across from him on a love seat. I never knew what to say to him. I didn't want to talk to him. I felt like he didn't care anything about me or getting me better. He would talk to me in a deep, monotone voice.

"How are you doing?" he asked each time.

"This place is so wonderful, why don't you trade places with me?" I wanted to say out loud, but I was a good girl. I had to prove to my doctor that I was sane. I was, but he didn't think so. My head was just full of thoughts that I couldn't make go away. I couldn't sleep. Not one of the pills I took would give me the good, deep sleep I needed. All the medication probably counteracted with each other. Who knew? I just wanted to get out of this horrible place. How could I convince my doctor I wasn't crazy? This place was making me even more crazy than I was when I came here. What was really wrong with me? No one really seemed to know how to fix what was inside my head.

Whatever I asked my doctor, he would come right back at me with a question. Why would I ask him anything? He never answered. My doctor didn't know any answers. He didn't even act like he knew any. His deep monotone voice, his breathing—long breaths and deep breaths—were annoying. He would write on his paper; write, write, write. Almost the whole time I was in there he was writing. He would rarely even look up at me. I couldn't stand him. He would nod his head. I guess he would nod his head to make me think he was listening to the few words I said to him. I never got much of a response from him, so why should I say anything? I would sit as still as I could, mostly looking out the window right next to the big chair he sat in. I didn't like him anymore than the day I first stepped foot in his office four years ago. He never told me anything that gave me any hope that I would get better. What he didn't know was that he was going to be the doctor to the most difficult and craziest patient in this pathetic place.

He was gone almost as quickly as I went to the small room to have a brief session with him. We only had small talk. He never told me what it would take to get me better. He never told me anything I wanted to hear. Nothing was ever accomplished. I never felt better after I talked to him. I hated going in that room with my doctor. He didn't ever say much to me, other than I needed to stay a little longer when I asked when I could go home. I said hardly anything to him, either. He just didn't seem to care at all what I was going through. I was just another patient he had to come and see.

There was a pay phone on the wall right across from the room I went in when my doctor did come. I could use it to call my family, and I tried to call Mother one day from the pay phone. I put my quarter in, and I couldn't remember the number. I was getting frustrated. I wanted to talk to Mother. I kept trying to dial the number, but I couldn't get it right. Finally, I slammed the phone down and gave up. I couldn't even call Mother.

I was heavily drugged. I couldn't sleep. I couldn't do anything in this place. I had very strange and bizarre thoughts when my worst time of the day came, nighttime. If only light could just shine day and night. At least, during the day, I could walk around. I could go into the TV room, or sometimes go to the little patio areas when someone would unlock the door for me.

The day finally came when I got to go outside the locked door at the end of the hall past all the patients' rooms. I went out with a group of the other patients. Someone who worked here escorted us out. The grass was vividly green. I could see tall trees covered with their leaves. I could see the whole sky, not just a small area as I did when I looked up from the patio area. This was freedom; this was true freedom. It was beautiful. The sun hitting my face felt so magnificent. It wasn't hot. It wasn't cold, either. The smell was, oh, so fresh. I could see far away. All this space was wonderful. I don't know how long it had been since I had been able to go outside of this place. This was awesome. This was freedom; true freedom.

There was a greenhouse not far from the door we walked out of to go outside. The greenhouse was just a short walk to the right of the door we exited. We went in the greenhouse that had plants on shelves all around it. There were small plants and big plants. The person that had brought us out here watered the plants as all of us watched. The greenhouse seemed rather small once all of us gathered inside of it. The plants were beautiful, but I wanted out of there to get to the huge open space.

Straight-ahead from the door that led to the outside world was a running track. We were allowed to run around the track, and I ran around and around it. I ran fast and furiously. I felt as if I was running for my life. It turned out to be just what I needed. There were exercise stations around the track. One spot was the standing broad jump. I would stand perfectly still and jump as far as I could.

I felt like a little girl playing outside. There were other exercises where I could stretch, push and pull, and much more. I could run, skip, hop and jump. I was full of excitement going around the track. I didn't show my excitement or laugh out loud, though. I didn't show any emotions.

I ran around the track, stopping at each one of the exercise stations. The track became the highlight of everything at this place. It was definitely the place I wanted to be at all times.

Off to the left from the door we all had walked out was a gazebo. It was white, large, and pretty. There was a bench to sit on that ran all around the inside of the gazebo.

The track was my favorite of everything outside the door we walked out from. To be outside of this dreaded place was the best. I loved it. Then the time came when we had to go back inside. I had to go back to the sad, depressing, awful part of this place.

Anger was part of my every day. I desperately wanted out. I wanted to go far, far away from this horrifying place. How could I get out? When would I get out? I hated it here.

Mania had taken over me before I checked myself in this place. I was depressed after my divorce from Kyle. I went from being completely depressed to a manic episode. It had been slow coming on, but it finally took me to a place where I couldn't even function anymore.

I was becoming a patient none of the nurses or workers wanted to deal with, I'm sure. Mania was my company, and I did not want it anymore. I didn't want to take all the medication. I didn't want to be behind locked doors. I just wanted to go home, wherever home was. Nothing had changed since I came here.

I needed someone to be able to help me get my brain back on track. Then I could be me again. The person I was in my late teens, early twenties. My anger and frustration at being so sick of this place became my weapons with which I would fight with to overcome my mania. I was full of anger, but still Mother and Debbie had no idea what I thought or how I felt. I didn't talk to them much at all. I didn't know what to say to them or anyone in this place. I would just walk around while they were there. They would try to get me to sit down at one of the tables in the family room with them, but I didn't want to even look at them.

Debbie gets so close to my face and looks in my eyes like she knows I'm there, but she doesn't seem to know how to bring her sister back to reality. I wanted her to get away from my face. And why was I so angry with Mother? I didn't want to face her. I didn't want her to see my face. I didn't want her to sit beside me. Oh, Mother, how hard this must be for you.

Melody

Melody

Melody

Melody

Daddy, Mother, Debbie, Teresa
and Melody

Momma Phillips, Debbie, Teresa
and Melody

Nonnie

Mother, Debbie, Teresa and Melody

Tara and Kayla

Trey

Tara

Kayla and Jadeyn

Trey

Tommy and Melody

LET ME OUT

I was going into the TV room more often now. I wanted to watch the news. I was very interested in what else was going on other than what was going on in this awful, boring place. As I watched and listened to the news, I was very attentive to every word. Where were all these things that were talked about on the TV happening? All I knew was that I wanted to hear it all. My mind was confused by all of it. I didn't know what or where they were talking about. It was somewhat of an escape from all that was done and talked about inside the walls where I was secluded.

At this point of my confinement, I was becoming worse than I was when I checked myself into this place. My behavior became uncontrollable. This place was awful to me. I would make the nurses and workers dread every day that they saw me, I'm sure.

I smoked a lot of the cigarettes Mother brought me. She had brought me a carton. Everyone's cigarettes were kept behind the nurses' bar and had our names written on our pack with a black marker. The nurse would bring out a plastic container full of everyone's cigarettes and set them at the corner of the nurses' bar each morning. I had to go to the bar and get a cigarette out of my pack if I wanted to smoke one. I had just one pack of my cigarettes in the plastic container, and a lighter was in there to light them. I had to put the cigarettes and lighter back in the plastic container after I lit my cigarette. Of course, I could only smoke in the family room and in the small patio areas.

I would sit down at one of the round tables and smoke my cigarette. It was great to have my own cigarettes. Cigarettes had been a bad habit of mine for a long time, since I was thirteen. I felt a little relaxed and a little calm smoking my cigarette, and I wanted a cigarette often. I would go to the bar, get my cigarette, light it, put my pack back in the plastic container, and sit at a table. At times, I would walk around with my cigarette from table to table. I had to ask the nurse each time if I could have one. I began to ask for a cigarette more often. I would smoke some of it and leave it burning in an ashtray. I would go to the bar, ask for another cigarette, smoke some of it and leave it burning in another ashtray. It wasn't always the same nurse that gave out the cigarettes to everybody. It would be whichever nurse was sitting behind the bar right in front of the plastic container. I would ask for a cigarette before I would finish the one that I had just gotten. When I would get another one, I would sit at another table and smoke it. The nurses found out I had cigarettes burning in one ashtray and another burning in another ashtray. A lighter for us to light our cigarettes had now been tied onto a thick wire, hanging down behind the bar. That change was to ensure that none of us could just get the lighter out of the container and possibly keep it; nor would anyone be allowed to light one after another, like me. I couldn't freely light my cigarettes anymore with the lighter that originally just sat inside the plastic container.

I was getting angrier because I couldn't get out of this place. I started acting like an uncontrollable maniac. I would walk around saying a phrase, walk that walk, talk that talk, snapping my fingers; just like the girl that I had seen doing that when I first came in here. When I saw her, I thought she was really strange. Now I was doing it. I would say stupid things that I thought were funny. I would laugh and twirl around.

I would say to Mother and Debbie, "I could've been a comedian."

I would laugh ridiculously, until I would be standing up with my legs crossed to try to keep from peeing in my pants.

When I would start laughing so hard Mother and Debbie would say, "Melody, go to the bathroom." I would sometimes just stand there. Other times I would run to the bathroom.

I was asking the nurses if I could check myself out often now.

"No, you can't," they all told me.

"Why? I checked myself in here," I would say to them.

Again, I was told I had to talk to my doctor about that. I never got anywhere with the doctor. He would not let me out and set me free.

If I would remember to ask him when we were in our chat room, all he would say to me is, "You have to get better. You have to stay a while longer."

I wondered how long. Would I ever get better? Would I ever get to the point when my doctor would let me out? Would all my days for the rest of my life be living behind these locked doors, in this place that had filled me with rage?

I was truly going even more nuts in this place. I was acting strangely before I came in this place. Now I was just infuriated about it all.

I'm crazy, I thought, or do you really call it crazy? Do you call it insane, or do you call it a chemical imbalance, or did I have a behavioral problem. After all, this entire place was a rehabilitation and behavioral center. I wasn't an alcoholic; I wasn't addicted to drugs. What kind of problem did I actually have? I definitely didn't know. I was just there, and I could not get out.

I hate my thoughts at night. I hated being locked in here and not even being able to go beyond the doors of this place unless someone was right behind me or in front of me. I wanted to be able to go wherever I wanted to go. I wanted to leave this horrifying place. This was all as if I were in a continuous dream, a nightmare. Just get me better and let me out.

I would sit at one of the tables in the family room and look at the newspaper. I would find the ad saying: Get a divorce for ninety-nine dollars.

I would yell out, "I want a divorce; I want a divorce."

The weird thing was, I didn't remember Vick. The only time I did know of Vick was at night outside my window. When he was crawling on the ground, and Mother and her husband were on the horses saying to him, "Get out of here, and go on." I knew who he was out there, but oddly, I didn't know who he was any other time. I didn't realize he was my husband. There were just all sorts of twisted thoughts in my head.

I was confused about who my husband was. I knew I was married, but in my thoughts I was still married to Tara and Kayla's daddy, Kyle. He was my husband at the time, so I thought. When I would point to the ad in the newspaper and I would yell, "I want a divorce!" it was Kyle I was thinking of. I just wanted a divorce. I don't know why. I don't know why I thought of Kyle when I saw the divorce ad.

My behavior was beginning to be even more bizarre. I continued to be uncontrollable. I still had extreme energy. I couldn't concentrate on one thing for very long. My mind had one thought after another. I wasn't thinking about what I was doing. I was acting like I was out of my mind. I knew, though, I wasn't. I just knew I wasn't. I was normal; I knew it, so why was I acting crazy, and why was I different than I had ever been before in my life? I knew I was somewhere inside of me. It was as if I was holding on to myself. I would not let myself slip away totally; I couldn't. I wanted to live. I want to live a life outside of this place.

I would still try to walk out of my room at night. I didn't understand why I had to stay in my room. I couldn't sleep. It just made me mad. Every time of any night, I would try to go to the lighted family room.

"Melody, go back to your room," the nurse said.

I would go back to my room, turn around, and I would try it again.

"Melody, it's not morning yet," the nurse would say with frustration in her voice.

When would morning come? My nights were so long. I didn't stop trying to get out of my dark room to get to the lighted family room. I could not have the light on in my room because I would be disturbing the other patients.

"Melody, we're going to have to give you a shot," one of the nurses said to me one night.

Was this supposed to scare me? Nothing here scared me at this point. If anything, they were probably scared of what my next move would be. I didn't care if they gave me a shot; I wanted them to, in hopes it would make me relax, or sleep so that my mind would stop racing. That night, a male nurse came in my room. He had a syringe in his hand. I was just standing there beside my bed. I knew he was going to give me a shot. I turned my back to him and I lowered my pants slightly so he could stick the needle in my hip.

"Go ahead, stick it in right here!" I said to him as I pointed to my hip.

The medicine in the syringe was to make me sleep, I thought. He gave me a shot in my hip and walked out of my room. Afterwards, I just lay in my bed kind of groggy, with my mind still racing. I would have loved for it to have knocked me out completely, make me sleep, and stop the thoughts that came one after another.

In my bathroom, I had a few washcloths. I would fold my washcloths in what looked to me to be the shape of babies. That was what they were to me. I would place my babies next to each other. I would hold them. I would move them from one place to another in my room. I didn't talk to them, I just had them there with me. I played with them like a child would play with her baby dolls.

I continued asking if I could check myself out. It still never was an option. They wouldn't let me out of the insane prison I was in. I was determined to get out. I knew I was in a place I did not want to stay in any longer. By this time I was fighting for my life. My life I wanted to live away from this place. I knew I could have a life out in the real world, if they would just let me out.

Some of the men in this place looked to be the age my daddy would be now, about fifty-five years old. I would see one of these men, and I knew it was daddy.

One day I saw a man escorted by a nurse along a hall I had never walked down. It was to the right side of the nurse's bar.

As he began to walk through the hall, I yelled out, "Daddy, Daddy."

The man went down the hall to a room where I would eventually go. I did not know yet why the room was there.

My friend Tracy was there visiting me that day.

I said to her, "Look Tracy, there's my daddy."

"No, he must just look like your daddy." He's not your daddy, Melody," she assured me.

I didn't argue with Tracy. My thought was that Tracy was always honest with me, and she would tell me if he were my daddy. Tracy had convinced me that the man was not my daddy. When she told me he wasn't, I then knew that the man I wanted to be my daddy was not him. I would love to see daddy and talk to him. I had never had a real conversation with Daddy; I only remember Daddy saying a few words around me.

There was a piano in the family room that was against the back wall. I would sit on the piano bench and play. I thought I could play really well. I had never played the piano in my life, other than trying to play as a child, the way young children do. I told Tracy I could play the piano, and she actually believed me. I was very serious and convincing.

Two songbooks lay at the top of the piano. They were church hymnals, full of songs I loved to sing in church when I was a young girl. They were the good "ole time gospel" songs. I loved those songs.

I would pick up one of the hymnals and let it fall open. I would prop it up on the piano. Whatever the hymnal fell to is the song I would play. I would play it for Daddy. I would think of Daddy as I played the song. I saw a picture of him in my mind. I saw smiles on his face, and I saw him laugh. I saw him and I standing up singing in church as we had done one Sunday morning. I would think of the day that I gave him his birthday present when I was thirteen. I remembered the hug I gave him and the words I said to him: "I love you." I would see his face with the expression he had when I gave him his present. He seemed to have had sadness in his eyes that day. He didn't say anything to me when I told him I loved him. He had simply accepted my hug and heard my words, then turned and walked away. I wondered what his thoughts were. I knew he did love the hug, and he loved hearing me say the words I told him. It was if all he could do was walk away. I knew in my heart that day that Daddy loved me, but he just could not say the words back. He looked as though he could cry.

I would open the other hymnal that was on top of the piano and prop it up on top of the one from which I played the song for Daddy. I would play a song for Mother from this hymnal. This one was Mother's hymnal. I would play songs for Daddy and songs for Mother. I would play a song out of Mother's hymnal, and, as I played the song for her, I would see her in my mind singing and smiling in our church choir. I would see her standing in front of our church, swaying back and forth as she signed to the deaf people who sat in the pews in front of her. She was always so beautiful when she sang in church. Whether it was singing in the choir, or singing and signing to the deaf people she loved so dearly, she was beautiful. I would let myself get lost in playing songs for them. I felt like I was the only person in the family room. Who knows what it sounded like? Just a banging sound like someone was trying to make a tune from it. I played them beautifully, though, so I thought. It made my heart full of joy. This was the only time I felt at peace in this place. Just thinking of Mother and Daddy when I played the songs that sounded beautiful to me filled my heart with happiness.

Mother and Debbie still came every day to see me. They would say anything to cheer me up. The thing was, there wasn't any cheerful thing they could say that could do it. They would talk to me, looking in my eyes to find out what was in my mind. They seemed to want to know the thoughts I was having. They could not figure out why I was in the sad shape I was in. Why couldn't they help me? They didn't know what to do. They never gave up on the day they hoped would come, though, when I would get out of this place. When would the day come that I would be the daughter and sister they knew I was? They missed seeing the person I was before all this happened to me.

Mother and Debbie would walk me out to the patio areas. They always had to ask a nurse to unlock the door before we could go out. I would sit and smoke. They would talk to me. Debbie would say to me, "Isn't it a beautiful day?"

I would nod, and just look up at the sky. She would sit with me while I smoked. I loved being outside.

When the time came to go outside, all the patients lined up at the back door and waited for the door to be unlocked. We were able to go outside again to freedom for a short while. My favorite thing to do each time I went outside was to run around the track. I ran and ran and did the exercises every time I went out there. I never got tired. I thought I could have run, jumped and stretched forever.

Some of the patients and I were escorted outside and were led beyond the gazebo one day. We came upon two wooden poles in the ground that had a wooden beam across them. The beam was twenty feet or so, and a rope was hanging down from the wooden beam. Everyone who wanted to try to climb it, could. I felt so brave and strong. Climbing up the rope would be no problem for me. It was a challenge and a risky thing to do. I couldn't wait to climb it.

It was my turn. I grabbed the rope and placed my hands around it very tightly. I looked all the way up to the top of the rope. It was exciting. As each one of them climbed up, the others cheered him or her on. The same cheering came from them when I was climbing the rope. I could do this, and I knew I would succeed. There were knots tied on the rope far enough apart to grab hold of them all the way up. I reached for each knot on the rope to help me climb up. I wasn't afraid of falling; the thought never crossed my mind that I could fall. I made it to the top with everyone down below cheering for me. When I got to the top, there was a small metal circle. To get down, I had to grab it. When I grabbed it, I flew down a trolley that took me back down to the ground. It was such a rush. I loved it. Climbing the rope was almost as good as the track, but that was the first and last time I climbed the rope. It was a big accomplishment for me. I felt so strong. There was nothing that could stop me from doing anything I wanted to do. I could do it all. I did everything I was allowed to do out in my area of freedom.

I was so bored inside. Nothing ever changed in here. I would do things that would get me in trouble. I once set off the fire alarm. I don't know what they said or did to me when I did that.

I was given pills and pills, more and more pills. All those pills I took never helped me get better. I wasn't making any progress in my treatment. I just continued to get worse and worse. I was sick of the nurses and the workers here. They had total control of everything in this place. They had complete control over me. I despised all of them.

The nurses seemed to become more and more annoyed at me. All I heard from them was, "Take your medication," "You've got to eat," and "You've got to wait to go to the patio." "You can't come out of your room until morning." "You can't check yourself out of here." "You've got to talk to your doctor." It all made me so very angry.

Once, I crossed the line. I went behind the nurse's bar. I didn't care that they told me I could not come back there. I was tired of being told what to do and when to do it. I was tired of them telling me "You can't do that." I was tired of them telling me "I could not check myself out." I went around the corner of the bar and slammed my arm down on it. All their papers about each one of us here were scattered across the bar. I slid my arm across it, and all of their precious pieces of paper went onto the floor. All the papers that documented what medication we were to take, when to give it to us, and whatever else they decided to put in our medical charts. The papers went up in the air and all over the floor. That was one of the many ways I showed them they were not going to win over me. I didn't think about what they would do to me; it didn't even matter. They treated me as if I didn't have a mind that could even function. I did, though. I would do unruly things to make them think I was just as crazy as they thought I was. I would be uncontrollable as long as I was in this place, as long as I had to. No matter what they did or said to me, I knew I was not crazy. I acted like a crazed person, but they didn't know I still had a mind that I would keep and never let go of.

None of them cared how I felt or seemed to want to help me. If they did, I could never see it in their eyes. I had a feeling they didn't even want to help me, or show me any kind of compassion. Someone could have just sat down and tried to talk to me. They were all heartless and cold. None of them ever said any kind words to me. I was a freak that nobody wanted to have anything to do with.

There was only one nurse I liked. She was very pretty and petite, with short, blonde hair that always looked like she just stepped out of a beauty shop. She was always in a good mood. She was the only one out of all of them who even smiled at me. Her voice was soft and sweet, and I wondered what she was doing here. She wasn't here very often, but, when she came, I felt as if she could rescue me out of this place. I loved seeing her.

I still did not know what day it was. I never knew and didn't even think to ask what time it was. What was the purpose of knowing? It was still the same every day. I didn't have a day to look forward to. I was never told I'd be able to go home soon. All I was told is that I'd have to stay awhile longer. Regardless of how much time had past or how many days I had been here, my answer to anyone who asked was still the same.

"I've been here two weeks," I would say, not knowing any different. Time stood still for me. The time never went beyond two weeks.

I don't know what kind of side effects I had from all the medication. Who could know? There were so many different ones. Would I still be acting insane if they didn't give me so many pills to take? I was heavily drugged. I never got sluggish, though, except the time I had that kidney infection. I still had extreme energy. I was a wound-up top that never could stop. I wanted to knock down the walls of this place and run to my freedom. I just wanted to be beyond locked doors. I don't know how I was being able to go on and on. I need rest and sleep, but rest and sleep was not possible for me.

I was standing in my room when a nurse walked in one day. She had braids all over her head. There were beads all through her hair, and she had a gold nail on her pinky finger. This nurse was mean. She was the worst nurse of them all. She dragged her feet when she walked. It sounded like she was wearing slippers. I could hear her beads clacking together. I always knew when she was here. I didn't even have to look up. I could tell by the noise of her clattering beads and her feet shuffling across the floor. I hated that sound.

When she came in my room she said to me, "You need to take a shower."

The only time I knew that I was going to take a shower was the time I was given the third degree when asking for a razor. I don't even know if I took a shower that day after asking for the razor. I know, though, I needed to groom myself. I'm sure I did need a shower. There's no doubt I looked pathetic. I probably had an awful odor, too.

The nurse said to me this time, "You are going to take a shower," with eyes that looked as if she could choke me.

"O.K. I will," I replied.

"You're going to do it now," she said, with the anger getting more intense in her voice.

She came close to me and got right in my face. She started taking off my shirt. I was mad at her. She didn't need to undress me.

With anger in my voice, I yelled, "I can do it by myself!"

"No, you can't," she said firmly.

She began to get rough with me. I was trying to prevent her from taking off my shirt. I wanted to hit her in the face with my fist. She was strong and tough, with a stocky build. I hated the sight of her. I felt it was not her place to be so forceful with me. She had her hands wrapped around my arms holding on to me with a tight grip. She squeezed my arm and was hurting me, now. She did not give me a chance to take off my clothes by myself and take a shower alone. I was furious, but I knew I could not stop her or fight her off.

She roughly took my shirt off, then my pants and my panties, throwing my clothes on the floor. She yanked me in the shower, holding me there, and then turned on the water. While the water flowed over my body, she got a wash cloth, soaped it up, and began to scrub my body hard. Her hair was swinging from one side to the other while those beads in her hair were clacking. The look on her face was as if she were saying, "You're no good for nothing." I just turned my head so I did not have to look into her empty, cruel eyes.

My body was weak as I stood in the shower feeling so invaded. I was tense at first, and then I just let my body go limp. After she had scrubbed my body, she put shampoo in her hand and started scrubbing my head just as roughly as she had scrubbed my body. My head was going in all different directions. As my body was limp, I just allowed her do her scrubbing. No matter which way she pushed and tugged me, I could not do anything. She pushed and pulled me while she held on to my arm with a very hard grip. Please, just let this be over.

She put my head under the showerhead. The water and the soap were running down my face. I wanted to cry, but I didn't. The tears wouldn't come. After she had finished scrubbing me, she pulled me from the shower. She grabbed a towel and dried me off. She was being very rough as she rubbed all the water off my body. She was just as rough with the towel as she had been with the wash cloth.

I wondered why she wouldn't try to talk to me in a tone that might have calmed me. I wondered why she couldn't be polite and tell me something like, "Let me help you take your shower," before she decided to push and pull me in every direction. She was just immediately angry with me. I really did want to do something all by myself. I needed some encouragement to be able to take a shower. After all, I did want to be clean. I had just forgotten that bathing was something I needed to do daily. I had no help from any of them to make a routine of doing the natural things I was supposed to do, like brushing my teeth, washing and brushing my hair; the things that I had forgotten to do day to day.

It was finally over. Why had she been so mean and hateful to me? She didn't have to treat me like I was a rag doll, trying to show me she had all power to do whatever she wanted to me. This was by far the worst thing that had happened to me yet. However, the very worst was still yet to come.

One night I was escorted down the hall I had seen the man walk down that I thought was Daddy. I barely got into the hall when the person escorting me through an unlocked door that was to the right of me. This was the room I had not known was here.

I was led inside this room, which was maybe ten feet by ten feet. The walls were painted white. There was a mattress that looked like an oversized baby mattress on the floor in the far right corner that lay against the wall. The vinyl-covered mattress was not covered with a sheet or a blanket. Why was I brought to this room? This person had me lie on the mattress. I didn't fight it. I had learned my lesson from the scrubbing I had gotten in the shower. I could not stop them from doing anything they wanted to do to me. I knew I could not prevent it.

After I lay down on the mattress, my hands were cuffed. Next, it was my ankles that were locked down in cuffs. The person who had placed me in this room had locked my hands and feet so I couldn't move. Then, I was just left there alone. I didn't even notice this person's face. I didn't care to look at this person at all.

I lay there looking around the room after the door had been locked. The only thing in here was the vinyl mattress and me, with my hands and feet locked in cuffs. I lay there somewhat calmly. I was tired. I was so mentally tired. I suppose they were teaching me a lesson. But what had I done to deserve this? I didn't know why I was put here. Was it because I had slung the nurses' papers off the lowered counter that was connected to their bar? Was it because the nurse got so angry with me when she gave me my shower? These questions didn't enter my mind until much later. Right now, I was just put away here for some sort of punishment, I guessed.

What did they expect from me? I was still heavily drugged. This place had made me become even crazier than I was when I checked myself in here. I was locked in here. I had no hope of getting out. How did they think I was supposed to act? I didn't know how I was supposed to act or respond to anything here.

I was seeing all sorts of people wanting to get some help. That's why we were all here. Some of the patients walked around like total zombies. Some people just sat at a table almost all day long. Where could we escape from the monotony of this place? We were locked behind the closed doors here without hope. My hope of leaving this place was long gone. If there were hope in any of these people, I didn't see it. The faces I saw in this place were long and sad, with emptiness in their eyes. We were not criminals. We were sufferers of depression, drug abuse, alcohol abuse, mania, heartache and despair.

This place was to help us learn what to do to get past our mental state we were in. If this place was helping any one of us, it definitely wasn't me. The only thing I was learning was to take pills, to feel hopeless, to feel loneliness, and to be crazy. I had come into this place with strange racing thoughts and bizarre behavior. My family had no idea how to help me. My family had to turn somewhere else for help. They put their trust in my doctor to bring me back to the person I once was.

As I lay on this hard mattress, I began to try to get my wrist free from the cuffs. I had lost so much weight, that I was now small and very skinny. Only flesh covered my bones; however, I was not aware that my weight had dwindled away. I was now eighty-something pounds. I had no idea what I looked like.

I have small wrists, so my wrists now were even smaller. I twisted my wrists back and forth. I pulled them slightly as I twisted to get my right wrist out of the cuff. My left wrist was next to the wall. I was not twisting and pulling fast or hard, as I had tried at first. I was getting nowhere in trying to get my wrist out like that.

My focus was completely on getting my wrist free from the cuff. I was twisting my wrist slowly as I pulled slightly to work its way out. I was making progress now. There was not one sound in this room. There was complete silence. In the position I was in, I had only one thought. It was to get free from my confinement. I had complete determination. My right wrist finally came through the cuff. I began to focus with the same determination on my left wrist. I was not making a sound. My thought process was only on succeeding to get both my wrists out of the cuffs. I was calm and very intense. I'm not sure how I was able to be so focused now. My left wrist finally came through the other cuff.

I was now sitting up working on my right ankle, with help from my hands. Then, someone unlocked the room. Someone entered the room where I lay. This person unlocked the cuffs from my ankles. I was escorted out of the room that had left me mentally deranged with a totally blank mind. My mind had focused to fight with determination to free myself. I don't know how I lay cuffed on that mattress without pulling and twisting my wrists until they were bleeding or bruised. My mind was still in tact. Maybe by just a thread, but that thread kept me fighting for myself so the thread would not break completely.

I do not know how long I had been in this room. I wished I had never come to know this room. It was punishment. I still did not know why I had been put in isolation; that was so cruel. How was I to know what would keep me from this punishment again since I didn't know the reason I had been put in solitary confinement in the first place? What would they do to me that could be any worse than this? Again, I do not know what was done with me after they let me out of this room, just as I did not know what they did with me after the cruelty of that nurse who had roughly made me get in the shower.

Mother and Debbie were, of course, still coming to visit me, but I never saw Teresa. I don't know what would have happened to me if they had not come to see me day after day. I had no clue what was going on with me. They knew what I didn't know, and that was that I was severely mentally ill.

I cannot ever understand how Mother, Debbie, and Teresa coped with what was happening with me. They prayed to God to help me and to help them. They knew in their hearts that their faith in God and the prayers that they lifted up to God would bring me back. Mother and Debbie were there for me day after day. They, nor Teresa would never give up on me. They would do anything in their power to get me to come back to reality.

THE OTHER SIDES

One day I noticed the hall that led to the chat room where I talked with my doctor continued past that room. I walked down the hall, and I came to some double doors at the end of it. The doors had long metal bars across them to push them open, and I pushed gently on one of the metal bars, but, of course, they were locked. There was a window in each door. The windows had crisscross lines on them. I did not know the windows were like this so they could not be broken.

I put my forehead to the window and cupped my hands around my face so I could see better. Beyond the doors, the hallway continued. I saw people on the other side of the doors. Why were there people over there? I could see what looked like to be a bar a short way from the doors where I was. The bar was not a long bar like we had over here; it a square shape. As I watched the people through the windows, I could see them walking around. I could tell they were talking to each other. I thought it must be better on the other side of the one I was in.

I would go to the double doors often now during the day. I was very intrigued about this other side, and I wanted to see all of it. Why were those people over there? Watching them became a sort of entertainment for me. The people looked happy over there. They mingled amongst each other. They talked and laughed. This side I was in was full of sadness, with no laughter except occasionally from the nurses.

I saw Debbie over there. Yes, I knew it was her. What was she doing on the other side? How did she get there? Why couldn't I go over there? Debbie talked to the other people. She laughed with them. As she walked around their bar, my eyes followed her. It was a soap opera over there. When I realized that's what it was on the other side, I was really mad at Debbie. How could she do this to me? She knew I was locked in this side. She knew I couldn't be a part of the other side. She was dressed up, and she looked very pretty. I hated my side. I hated it so much. I hated it even more knowing Debbie was on the other one. It was fun over there. My side of this place was horrible.

The next time Debbie came to see me, I didn't want her to look at me. I didn't want her to be here. When she was on the other side, she was happier than she was with me. She didn't laugh at all with me. She always got very close to my face to talk to me. She had no idea I thought she was in a soap opera on the other side.

Once, when Mother and Debbie came, they took me to another side that was in this place. I was actually allowed to go beyond the side I was locked in. I didn't know where I was going with them. I still was not talking to them when they came to see me. I didn't ask where we were going. I had a strange feeling as I walked with them. I just looked around in amazement that my side was not the only place here.

We went through the doors that led to a big cafeteria. When we walked into the cafeteria, there was a line of people there, and we got in the line behind them. We were all in line to get to a spread of food. We each got a food tray that we slid down across the metal poles attached in front of the food. This place was like a school lunchroom. When we got to the food, there were three or four people behind the layout of food. Everyone told them what they wanted, and they put the food on a plate for each of us. All the food looked delicious. I didn't know what to choose to eat. I actually felt hungry for the first time in I didn't know how long. I hadn't seen good food like this in a while.

Mother and Debbie asked me, "What do you want to eat?"

I didn't know what I wanted. I couldn't make a choice all by myself.

"Do you want this?"

I just stood there kind of shrugging my shoulders.

"How about this? This looks good."

I would shake my head yes or no, and they were telling the lady what to put on my plate. They had all kinds of desserts, and I did choose a piece of pie.

I looked around this cafeteria. I felt a little out of place, and somewhat strange. I couldn't believe all the people that were here. I didn't want anyone to look at me. We sat down at a long table, where there were about five or six people sitting. I just looked around observing everything and everyone, like I so often did.

I started eating my food, and I liked it; it all tasted great. This was much better than sitting on my side of this place and eating whatever they brought for me. I had always sat and eaten alone on my side, except when Mother or Debbie were there. This made me want to eat, since there were other people around me who were enjoying eating. The people were talking and laughing as they ate. People looked happy. Gosh, I wanted to have that feeling that everyone else seemed to have. I wanted to feel happy, and I wanted to be able to laugh like they were. I had gone without having hardly any desire to talk, or smile, or laugh the whole time I'd been here. It was good to see the people enjoying their food and their conversations with one another. I was in a pleasant surrounding.

I was able to look at people's faces now as I sat beside Mother and Debbie. I was not hiding my face now. I felt a little more at ease now when someone looked at me. I was even able to smile at a couple of people who looked at me.

I did feel a little out of place and somewhat nervous sitting around so many people. I watched people walking to chairs. I watched people talking and eating.

There were huge windows that took up almost the whole wall to the left of the tables. I gazed out the windows. I saw so many cars out there, and I wondered whose cars they were. I wanted to go out there, get in one of those cars, and leave.

Was everyone watching me the way I was watching them? I didn't know how to act. Where were all these people from? None of the faces were familiar to me.

When Mother, Debbie, and I were through eating, we put our trays at a counter, just like in school. The trays were placed there so they could be cleaned, the same way in a school cafeteria. I was now aware of another side of this place.

I was given the privilege to go to the cafeteria side twice. I lost my privilege, though. I threw food everywhere one day when I got there. I don't know why I starting throwing my food. Maybe it was the anger and frustration that had became part of my everyday living. I now had to be confined to the family room again to eat. I went back to having my tray brought to me. I didn't get to have the good food that was at the cafeteria. Everything was the same as it was before I knew of the cafeteria side.

I desperately wanted to leave this place. Why wouldn't they let me out of this place? When I checked myself in this place, I thought I would get better. They told me I would be here two weeks, but that didn't happen. At the beginning of my stay, I tried to understand what this place was, but I never did.

I realized they would not let me out. It didn't matter how many times I asked to get out of this place. It didn't matter that I pleaded to my doctor to let me go home. None of them listened to my pleas. I would never have any control over what I wanted to do. My doctor, the nurses, and the workers had all control over me, and I was sure they always would.

A group of us lined up and were led to yet another side one day. As we walked down a long hall in a line, I saw there were windows to the left. I looked out, and there were buses parked outside. They were short buses, like mini vans. As I walked, I stared at the buses. I knew why the buses were here. They were going to transport the bad people out of here and take them to a place even worse. It gave me a shiver. I feared that a day might come when I would be loaded up on one of those short buses and carried away from here. I was afraid I would be tortured even more if they took me to another place.

We arrived at the room we were being led to. It was a room full of crafts and all sorts of things people had made. I looked on the shelves on each wall as we walked down a short hallway. This place was great. I was amazed that people had made things out of wood, leather, clay, and paint. Past the short hallway, we walked in to a huge room. There were tables long enough for everyone to have a seat. We were to select something we wanted to make. I wanted to make everything that was in here. There were tee-shirts to paint designs on, and I finally decided what I wanted to make.

I chose a dark pink tee-shirt to paint. I sat down and began to choose a tube of the color I wanted to use. I was enjoying myself as I sat and painted on my tee-shirt. My mind was not racing as much anymore. The racing thoughts were beginning to slow down. I was determined to do a good job painting my tee-shirt. Choosing what I wanted to make all by myself made me feel confident. I was able to make a choice and a decision to do something.

Tara and Kayla never really entered my mind. I didn't wonder where they were, or what they were doing. I was deciding what to paint on my shirt. I chose a tube of silver paint and dribbled it around on the shirt. As my hand moved across the shirt, I dribbled the silver paint from the tube. When I finished painting it, there was my little girl's name. I had written "Kayla" on my tee-shirt.

It was time for us to leave now. I had to leave my shirt in the craft room. I didn't know what would happen to it, but it was left in the craft room with all the other things people here had made. Some of them weren't finished, and some of them were. Were the people that were making or had made all these things going to be able to get them? Why were they still here in the craft room?

I was finding out there were so many sides to this place. For so long, I thought my side was the only place here. There was another side I was led to on another day. Now, someone was leading me each day to greener pastures. I just followed my leader in line with the other people who were being led.

This place I lived in was actually huge, with many sides. We reached a big room that had several chairs facing a marker board. I felt like I was in school, now. I was in a classroom with the other people, and a female teacher stood at the front of the room by the marker board. She began to talk and write words on the marker board, but I didn't put together the meaning of anything she was saying or writing.

I did what I normally did at whatever side I was in. I observed everything around me. Some of the chairs had no one sitting in them. All of us were scattered in the room in the chair we had chosen. I watched what the other people sitting close to me were doing. They were sitting still with their eyes on the teacher. They seemed to understand everything she was saying and writing.

I tried diligently to sit still. I was bored listening to the words the lady was saying. I wanted to write on the marker board. I wanted to stand up and walk all around the room. I had to make myself be still and try to listen to the teacher like I should in a classroom. I began to stare at the teacher; I heard no words coming out of her mouth. It was as if everything went silent. While I tried to focus on the words she was saying, all I saw were her arms and her mouth moving. I watched her walk back and forth in front of the class. I watched her write on the marker board. My mind was only focused on her movements, not what she was saying.

Each time I would leave a different side, I was always led back to my dreadful side.

I was having new adventures often now. On one of my adventures, I was led into a dark room. There were just a few other people besides me that went there. There were reclining chairs, and we were told to sit in one. This was the most comfortable spot I had sat in since I had been here. The lights were off. I didn't like the lights off. I wanted to see everyone in here. I wasn't able to do what I always do, watch and observe everyone.

As I lay in my recliner, someone began to speak in a monotone voice.

"Close your eyes; relax. Let your body go limp from your head to your toes," was coming from the monotone voice of this person.

Music was playing. It was the kind of music that was to help a person relax, but I couldn't relax. This was not an option for me. I didn't like this side. I began squirming around in my chair. I was snickering and making noises, disrupting this relaxation therapy. Then someone came and escorted me back to my side. I was actually relieved. I was not ready for that kind of therapy at all. I guess they figured that out. I was never taken to that little dark side again.

If I didn't focus on people, I was moving. I walked around the family room. I went in to the TV room. I would focus a little on what was on TV. If it wasn't news, I didn't want to watch it.

I would go in my room. I would move things around. There wasn't much in there to move around, though. Most of my clothes had been taken out of my room, so I didn't have access to those anymore. I unfolded and folded the few clothes I did have access to. I had had my purse when I first came in here. I would take everything out of my purse and then I would put it all back in. I would take out my pictures. I would rearrange them in each of the plastic sections I kept them in. I laid them in a line on my counter in my room. I would unfold papers I had in my purse. I would fold them back up differently. I would go through my purse like a fine toothed comb over and over. Eventually, my purse was taken away from me, too.

One day I was able go to the other side beyond the locked double doors. This was the only other side I had thought was here until I was able to go to the other ones. I was going to be in the soap opera. This is the day I had hoped would come. This side was just as I thought it would be. I was thrilled to be able to finally see it. I think I even managed to have a small, genuine smile come across my face.

My favorite nurse escorted me to this side. I only saw her occasionally, but I wished I could see her all the time. She was the prettiest one, and by far, the most compassionate one. Actually, she was the only nurse here who was nice to me. She was the best person out of everyone in this whole place. She was the one I always loved to see.

She walked in front of me holding her head high. She seemed to be completely dedicated to what she was and what she did. Her petite body, her blonde hair, her smile that made everything better. She was my angel here, and I loved her. She was the only person that made me feel good and gave me some hope of getting better and getting out of this place. Most of all, she treated me like a normal person. The other ones looked at me like I was completely out of my mind. I was in some ways, but I wasn't as out of my mind as they thought I was.

When my favorite nurse and I reached the bar on the other side, she began to talk to all the other people on this side. I followed her so proudly, like a child would with her mommy. She smiled and laughed with everyone. I stayed right by her side. She and I strolled through the halls and rooms here. I knew she knew a side of me that the other ones didn't. I just felt it inside. She seemed to be able to see the inner depths of me and believed I was not what they thought I was. I felt all through me that she knew I was not crazy.

We came up to a pool table. My nurse stood by me as I picked up a pool stick. I leaned over the pool table and looked at a ball. I focused hard on hitting the ball in one of the pockets. When I hit the ball, I wanted to jump up and down and laugh. That moment I felt like I had done something that no one else in this place would have allowed me to do—have a little fun.

My nurse didn't keep her eye on me every minute as we strolled through this side. She didn't have to. She knew I was good and sane in my inside self. My nurse took me to a place outside where several young people were sitting, who looked to be around my age. They were smoking, and just seemed to be hanging out. She talked to them, calling them by their names. She knew them. I wanted to stay on this side with all these people. It was fun over here. Why couldn't I stay on this side? I didn't see Debbie here. I realized it was not a soap opera. The other side was real, just as real as my side.

I would never be allowed to stay on this other side. Over there, people had problems, too, but they were all so far ahead of me in their progress in getting better. I never reached the level I needed to so that I could stay on the other side.

I had to stay on the worst side of them all. There wasn't any progress with me. I only went farther and farther down hill. As time went by, I became worse.

I did enjoy going to the craft room. It was good therapy for me. But I still hated the path we took to get there. The fear of being taken away in one of those short buses never went away. I thought about that every time I walked past them. The craft room was the only therapy that worked for me except when I was outside running around the track. Of course, the side I longed for always, was the outside.

MORE BIZARRE THOUGHTS
AND BEHAVIOR

I was allowed to go on weekend passes now. I might have been able to leave so that the nurses could get a break from me, or maybe they wanted to find out how I would act outside of this place. Either way, if it was to help me or to give them a break, I had now become able to get away from this place.

Mother took me to a flea market with her during one of my weekend passes. It was a workout for Mother to keep up with me. I was looking around everywhere at this market. I was trying to go this way and that way. Mother talked to me like I was a small child. Many times, my behavior was like a small child. Mother tried to keep me close to her saying, "Stay with me. Come on, let's go this way." After the weekend was over, I had to go back to the hospital, the place I hated.

I went on a weekend pass with Vick once. I couldn't quite figure out where I was, or why I was with him. He took me to the trailer house we lived in before I went into the hospital. It had been moved to a different place, amongst several trees. I felt like I had been taken far away. The trailer was dirty, so I picked up a broom to sweep the floor. It was a very strange place, and I was confused. Is this where I'm going to be now? It seemed like I was only there for a very short time. That weekend pass was not a good experience. I hated the hospital, but I didn't want to be here at this trailer house.

I went home again with Mother on another weekend pass. Vick was at Mother's house. I still did not connect everything about Vick. I still did not realize he was my husband.

It was late at night and I was lying on the floor at Mother's watching TV. The news was on, and I listened to it intensely. I called Debbie on the phone.

"Debbie, there is going to be a war," I said to her very seriously.

I didn't pay attention to what she was saying back to me. I had to let Debbie know we were going to war. It was real to me. There was going to be a war. It was going to be our country battling against another country.

"Yes, Debbie, there is going to be a war," I said, knowing it was true.

Then I hung up the phone. This was just another one of the bizarre thoughts I had. Again, it was at night when this thought came to my mind.

I should have been excited to go on my weekend passes. It was mostly all the same to me wherever I was. I was always in my own world, a world I could not understand. I was still not able to tell anyone my inner, deep thoughts. I don't know why. Why should I tell anyone? How do I explain the way I am? I could not find the words to say. I really never thought about telling anyone. This was the way I lived my life now. My head was full of all sorts of horrible, crazy, bizarre, and unusual thoughts. I could not get them out of my head. My family, my doctor, nor the nurses knew what I was battling with.

I knew I was somewhere deep inside myself. The problem was that I didn't know how to bring myself out and be the way I was before mania came my way. I knew my life was different before. My mind was broken.

I had no idea that I had an illness that was affecting my thoughts, my emotions, and my behavior. I never had a break from the craziness in my mind. I didn't seem to have any control over anything I thought or did. My doctor, Mother, Debbie, the nurses—none of them explained to me what was happening to me. If they did, I didn't know of it. I was out of reality day after day, week after week. I did not know the day of the week or the time of the day it was.

I never thought about brushing my hair, brushing my teeth, or what I looked like. All these things people do without much thought at all. I didn't do any of those things anymore, nor did I realize I needed to.

My behavior became worse as time went on. I began to take other patients' belongings from their rooms. I took their shoes, and other belongings of theirs. All of it was mine, I thought. I once took a lady's eyeglasses out of her room. I needed those eyeglasses; I couldn't see well. I needed glasses so I could see. I had been telling Mother and Debbie I couldn't see well, and I needed glasses. The glasses were taken away from me, and I was told they were not mine.

I was escorted to the isolated room again. The room I wished I had never come to know about. I was left alone in this room again. This time it was much different, although the over-sized baby mattress was still here with me. The difference this time was that my wrists and ankles were not put in cuffs. I had worked my wrists out of the cuffs last time. Maybe that was why I wasn't held down with them this time. I was horrified this second time of isolation. I was full of anger and rage. I was once again in the very worst room in this whole place.

I immediately started knocking and banging on the window of the door I was locked behind. The door was in the center of the wall, and this window was the same as the windows on the doors that led to the other side with the crisscross lines. It, too, was a window that was made not to be broken.

I yelled as I knocked and banged on the window.

"Please, please, let me out! Please!" I yelled, pleading for someone to come and let me out of this room.

I noticed another small window on the wall directly across from the locked door. There was a ledge at the bottom of this little window. I tiptoed to reach it. I placed my hands on the ledge. On the other side of the window, I saw two nurses. I began to knock and bang my hands on that window just as I had done at the window on the locked door.

I was yelling again, "Please, let me out! Please! I'll be good, I'll be good!"

I yelled these same words over and over. I was terrified. Would someone come and let me out?

I watched and pleaded with the nurses. I yelled and kept screaming. The nurses never looked up at me. The two of them were shuffling papers, and I could see they were talking between themselves. Do they hear me? Why am I in this room again? Why? They couldn't hear me, or, if they could they were ignoring me.

I went to the mattress and I picked it up. I pushed it up against the wall it was lying on the floor by. I pushed it until it was flush against the wall. Then I let it slam to the floor. I was infuriated. I picked up the mattress again and pushed it down to the floor. Each time I picked it up, I was slamming it down harder and harder. Bam! Bam! Bam! I was slamming it harder and faster each time. I was so outraged, and scared I might never get out of this room.

I went back to the locked door. I was banging on the window again.

I yelled the same as before, "Please, someone let me out! Can anyone hear me? Please, let me out! I'll be good! Please!"

I ran back to the small window the nurses were behind. I banged and yelled again. They still did not look up at me. Back to the mattress I went, picking it up and slamming it down, fast and furiously, slamming it over and over. No one cared what I was doing or what they were putting me through in this room. None of them could even hear me.

I went back to the door. This time I laid flat down on the cold concrete floor on my stomach. The door wasn't flush to the floor, and at the bottom of the door was a small crack. My whole body was stretched out on the floor with my head at the crack. I looked through the small crack and stuck my fingers through it as far as I could.

I yelled out from the crack, "Please! Let me out! Someone, please let me out! I'll be good! I'll be good!"

I wiggled my fingers, hoping someone would see them. No one did. If so, I never knew it. I was a crazed woman in this room, more so than any other time. My body never stopped going during the whole time I was isolated. My body was always rushing to keep up with my brain. My mind was racing with fear and anger the whole time I was in solitary confinement. I do not know the answers or reasons why I was going through any of this.

My experience in isolation was the worst treatment I could have ever gotten. I never would have believed people were actually treated in such a way. Yes, I was mental, but were people educated enough about mental illness? Didn't they realize we were normal people who had no control whatsoever of so many things we did? They did not know what was in my head.

Just as before, I don't know how long I was kept in isolation or what they did with me when they did let me out.

My mind became full of thoughts of God, now. I had not prayed to God in such a long time. I had not thanked God in a long time either. God was with me, but was I acknowledging God's presence?

My thoughts were very eerie now. I began to wonder if these people here knew of God. Who here was born again? Were any of them born again? They must be saved. They must have Jesus in their heart. They were going to hell if they did not believe and know this. If they were born again, they would go to heaven.

I began to be fearful for people, fearful they did not know God. I thought back through my life of people I knew—who was close to God, who I thought wasn't.

There was a marker board hanging on the wall in the family room. I had never noticed this marker board being there. What was to be written on it? I picked up a black marker when I noticed the board was there. It was a black, permanent marker. I wrote on the board with the marker, three big letters. The letters spelled the word GOD. I started writing peoples' names I knew. They were names of my family, my friends, and anybody's name I could think of whom I knew. The names I wrote were scattered around the three letters, GOD. Some of the names I wrote way up at the top of the board. Some I wrote down at the bottom of the board. I wrote "Roy" way up high on the board, above all the other names. Roy was my daddy's name. He was up in heaven, so that's why I wrote his name way up at the top of the board. Mother's name, Laverne, was up high on the board, too. I didn't put her name all the way at the top, though, because she was not in heaven yet. Her name was one of the names that was written at the top of the board because she was close to God. She always let it be known that God was the most important person to her. She was going to heaven.

As I wrote the names, I thought about how close to God each one of them was. I placed a name in the middle of the board. I wrote a name towards the bottom of the board. One by one, I wrote the names of people who came to my mind. All the names were people I had known through the years of my life. My name wasn't on the board. After writing so many peoples' names all over it, I never noticed the board again.

Each night now before going to my room, I walked past everyone's door to his or her room. We all had our names on the wall beside our doors. They were placed there, as all patients' names would be in a hospital. As I walked down the hall, I paused at each door. I would put my finger by each of the names as I came to them. I marked a check with my finger beside each name. I always put a check mark by every name. They were sure to go to heaven if a check mark was beside their names. I didn't want any of them left behind. I did this each night before going to my room.

It gave me a sense of peace after I placed a check mark beside each name. They would be safe now from the fire of hell. God would take each one of them when he came to take his people home.

DO THEY KNOW
HOW TO HELP ME?

I could no longer go to the cafeteria because I had thrown food everywhere. I wasn't able to freely have access to my cigarettes like I did at the beginning. I didn't realize I would leave one burning and yet I would ask for another one. I wasn't able to leave for a weekend. My weekend passes were no longer permitted. I don't know why they wouldn't let me leave for a weekend ever again.

I could not sit still in the therapy room where the recliners were in the dark. I disrupted the class with my squirming in my recliner and my giggling. I didn't like that room, anyway. It didn't make any sense to me to lie back and listen to a monotone voice. The voice was telling me to breathe and to relax and feel my whole body go limp. I couldn't find a picture in my mind that would give me peace and quietness like the voice told me to. This type of therapy just did not help me.

I was admitted here into the ICU ward for the worst mental patients. The other patients came into this unit and quickly moved on to their recovery. They went to the other side. The side I always wanted to be on. I didn't ever get to go beyond the ICU ward. I was not able to stop my bad behavior.

There wasn't anybody who knew how to help me overcome and get my mental illness controlled. My family couldn't help me. My doctor didn't know how to treat me. The nurses had long given up on me. Medication did not make me get any better. All the medications that were given to me to treat mental illness just made me worse. It was if I was an experiment they could not master.

Everyone had come to a dead end. All of them had no clue as to what was going on with me. They had no clue whatsoever what to do for me. I was mentally ill, but they could not determine which mental illness to diagnose me with.

There were more psychiatrists and psychologist brought in to try to figure out what was wrong with me. My doctor and the other doctors could not reach a solution to bring me out of the state I was in. Some of the doctors believed I was schizophrenic, some believed I was paranoid schizophrenic, and some believed I was psychotic. I had symptoms of all these mental illnesses. My doctor stood firm on what he thought I had. He diagnosed me with bi-polar disorder.

My family was told I might not ever overcome the state I was in. They were told that I might never be able to take care of my children. They were told I could die. My doctor recommended them to admit me into the state mental hospital.

I was a case that had been given up on. My mental illness was so severe, it was hopeless. My family was lost as to what to do now.

My stay went from a possible two weeks to a long three months. I made absolutely no progress; in fact, I was much worse now than I was when I checked into this hospital.

Mother would not accept what they were telling her. She would not give up hope. There was nothing that brought Mother down. If she fell down, it was to her knees to pray to God. She was so strong. God was her enter strength. Mother always knew and was aware of God's presence. She knew with all her being everything would be all right, because God took care of all things. That's how Mother lived her life, having faith and believing in God always.

After three very long months, this place was letting me leave. They finally let me out. I was beyond their ability to treat me any longer.

My insurance was maxed out. The insurance policy was not going to pay anymore for my treatment. There would be no more money paid to my doctor by the insurance company I was covered by, nor would there be any more money paid to the hospital. This place, the place that kept me for as long as my insurance paid, now wanted to send me on to a state mental hospital. How much money had the doctors and this place gotten? A tremendous amount, no doubt.

Mother made it clear that I would not be going to any state mental hospital. She was taking me home. She was told it would be a twenty-four hour, seven-day-a-week job, but Mother took the job on without hesitation. She would never give up on the possibility that her daughter would come back. She would do anything in her power to make that happen. God would be by Mother's side through it all. God's will would be done. He was in control of it all. I knew that was how Mother thought.

My brain needed rest. It never slowed down. I never got the sleep that was necessary to slow it down. It was unbelievable how I kept going. My body was full force, charged with energy. My body was racing furiously to keep up with my brain. My brain had been full of strange, eerie, bizarre, and out of the ordinary thoughts, and my thoughts continually raced through my mind.

I never told these thoughts to anyone all this time. I didn't let them out for anyone to hear. I wasn't purposely keeping them to myself, I just couldn't make any of them come out so that I could tell anyone. I didn't know why. I never thought about saying what I was thinking. My family never knew my thoughts all through this. I didn't know when or if they asked me what I was thinking. I don't know if my doctor or anyone else asked, either. I was in my own world. It was a world that everyone seemed to know little about.

Little did we all know that admitting myself in this hospital would not help me nor get me back to being a sane person. My doctor had no idea how to get me better. Maybe he tried, but he did not succeed.

HOME AT LAST

I was leaving the place where I had lived for three months. The place I had been begging to leave. I had said so many times after I checked myself in that hospital, "I want to go home."

My request had finally been granted. None of us had known if this day would ever come. It finally did because there was no other choice. Mother was taking me home with her.

Toward the end of my stay in the hospital, Vick had stopped coming to see me. He eventually stopped keeping in touch with my family. He was long gone when I checked out of the hospital. I hadn't known who he was, actually, through the whole time I was there anyway.

Mother had raised me and provided for all my needs. She loved me. I was her child. At the age of twenty-six, Mother was going to provide for all my needs again. She was going to do whatever it took for her child to get better. Her child was grown now, but had slipped back to child-like behavior. My mother was determined to bring me back to reality and out of the world I was in. She wanted me back with her.

My doctor was right. All of Mother's days now were spent keeping up with me. She had to watch almost my every move. I hadn't been home for very long when one day Mother noticed that I had been sleeping on the couch for a while. I had actually fallen into a good, deep sleep. I had not had slept like that in a very long time. Mother called my name. She tried to get me to wake up. After trying with no success, it frightened her. She called my doctor's office and left a message for him to call her. When he returned her phone call, she told him she could not wake me up. He told her this is what we've been wanting her to do all this time, sleep. Let her sleep.

I had slept for two or three days. My brain had gotten rest after all this time. All the many pills I had been given never got me to go into a good, deep sleep. They never made my mind slow down. Neither the pills nor the therapy had done what they were supposed to do for me.

Mother left the hospital with a big zip lock bag of pills that was given to her when she took me home. I continued to take several pills a day.

The medication, however, produced side effects. My body became so stiff that I walked like a soldier. My eyes bulged out of my eye sockets. When I lay in my bed at night, I could not roll over from my back to my side, because it was painful. I would call Mother to come turn my body so I could lie on my side. I could only lie on my side for a very short amount of time, and I would have to call for Mother to come turn me to my back again.

Mother let my doctor know of my body's stiffness. She was told the drug Cogenten I was taking had side effects that were causing those things. My doctor told Mother to stop giving it to me.

As time went on, I was taken off one pill after another. Mother was now being told not to give me this one anymore. She was told I didn't need this one or that one anymore. My doctor took me off all my medication. I did not continue taking any of them. I had a mental illness, but my doctor didn't keep me on any of the medication. I couldn't have been happier to stop taking pills. I was sick of taking so many pills. I no longer had to take even one of the many I had been prescribed.

While I was in the hospital, I know Mother got comfort from everyone at her church. She was going to the church I had grown up in. A lot of the people there had known me for years, and I know they all had prayed for me. I was so thankful for all their prayers; everyone had prayed for me, and God did answer their prayers. I was getting better now. I know Mother always knew in her heart that God and the people at church would keep her going, and they did.

I went to church with Mother one Sunday since I was better now. I couldn't get any meaning from what the preacher was saying. I couldn't concentrate on the sermon. It was difficult for me to sit still. I was not comfortable around so many people. As I sat in the church pew beside Mother, I was nervous and anxious. My heart was beating fast. I had to get out of there. I could not sit still in that pew any longer. I tried, but I couldn't. I told Mother I needed to go home. We had to leave before the sermon was over.

I went back to church again with Mother. Each time we went, I felt more comfortable. Soon I was enjoying church as I always had. I was praying again, and I was so thankful that I could feel God's presence again. I loved how I felt the Holy Spirit while I sang and listened to the preacher.

I wanted everything in my life to come back together. I wanted Tara and Kayla back with me. I was back in the real world now. My body had slowed down, and I was sleeping. The excessive energy, the bizarre thoughts and the out of the ordinary behavior had gone away.

My doctor wrote a letter that stated I was competent to have Tara and Kayla come back to live with me to give to the judge. The day they came back home with me was truly the most wonderful day ever. I was ecstatic to have my girls back with me. I had my life back on the right track.

I needed to get a job now. I wanted to go back to work, and I was well enough to be able to work again. I had to be responsible for Tara and Kayla and myself. I couldn't rely on Mother forever to take care of all my needs.

I received a phone call from one of the places where I had applied for a job. It was a cable company, and they needed someone for a customer service position. I was asked to come in for an interview. I did, and I was hired. It was a huge accomplishment for me to get a job. I would provide for Tara and Kayla and myself again. I was determined to do just that.

I made enough money now to be able to get my own place. I moved into a mobile home park. There were other kids there, so Tara and Kayla would have other children to play with. The mobile home I moved into was spacious, and I liked it. It would be a good place for us to live. Being able to get my own place was another big accomplishment for me. I felt really good now that I had a job and a place for my girls and me. We had our own home again, and it felt great.

A lady my age was my neighbor. She was a single Mom, too, and we became good friends. She would come over and visit me, and we talked and laughed. I was glad to have her around. I hadn't had a friend to talk to in quite a while.

I went to work, and Tara and Kayla went to school. I enjoyed my job, and I became good friends with some of my co-workers. Tara and Kayla did well in school. It was exciting to see all the school papers they brought home. Tara and Kayla went to their daddy's house every other weekend.

Sometime, we went to church Sunday mornings when they were with me. They loved going to church as I had when I was a young girl. They sang in the children's choir as I had. It made me so proud watching and hearing them singing in the choir in front of the church. I wanted them to learn more about God. They needed to know that God so loved the world that he gave his only begotten Son so that they might have eternal life, just as I had come to know. I wanted them to believe in that so they would have faith, hope, and love that would carry them throughout their lives.

I had overcome my episode of mania. I was living my life again.

Lost Years

I was still married to Vick. It had been a year since we had spoken. I didn't ever really think of getting in touch with him. It was time to file our income tax return, so I called him to ask what he wanted to do about it.

We talked for a short time, and I asked about Brittney and told him I would like to see her. I went to Vick's house when the weekend came. I saw Brittney and Vick and I talked. That same day, we decided to get back together. Vick moved in with me, and Brittney would come every other weekend.

Soon after we got back together, we talked about having a baby. I wanted to have another child. It wasn't very long at all before I was pregnant with my third child. I couldn't wait to have my baby and was very excited. I wanted to have a boy. I prayed that God would give me a son. I wondered if it was wrong to ask God for that. The important thing was to have a healthy baby.

I always wanted to have my children before I was thirty years old. I would be three months shy of thirty when my baby would be born. The baby bed was put up. We decorated the baby's room in pale blue and green, everything was all together and I was ready for the birth of my third baby.

In January my beautiful, healthy, baby boy was born. God had blessed me by giving me a son. We named him after his daddy and granddad. He was a third, so we called him "Trey." I was a proud mother once again.

Trey was such a good baby, just like Tara and Kayla had been. Tara and Kayla were happy to have a little brother. They held him and played with him, and they loved him. I had a complete family now. I had my three children just as I had always wanted.

A few years went by, and I found myself unhappy again. The ups and downs came again. It became difficult for me to enjoy life at times. At other times, I felt on cloud nine. I was down more than I was up most of the time. Depression came my way much more often than mania did.

When I was at work, I smiled, I talked, and I laughed. I worked very hard to be a good employee. I enjoyed working, and my job made me feel better about myself. I tried to be happy at home, but it was difficult. If anyone saw how I was at work, he or she would have never guessed I was depressed. It's odd that I could do my job and do it well being depressed. But my job was an escape from my depression. I was able to keep my moods good at work, but many days after getting home I was back to the unpleasant moods. There were days when as soon as I got home, I would go straight to my room and stay there in my bed for at least an hour or two. I didn't feel like talking to anyone. I would then get up, although, not wanting to, I needed to fix my family supper. Other days I would come home and enjoy spending time with my kids, and was talkative.

Vick and I moved about once a year. Tara and Kayla went to different schools each time we moved. I know it had to be hard on them to have to change schools so much. They would have to meet new friends and start over each time.

Kayla had been telling me for a while now that she wanted to go live with her daddy. She was eight years old now. I didn't want to let her go. I could see in her, though, that this was what she wanted. Kayla was always more of a daddy's girl. One night, when Kayla was telling me she wanted to live with her daddy, we got in the car and I took her there. I told him she wanted to live with him. That night was the night I let her go. I didn't know if I had made the right decision, but if this was what it took for Kayla to be happy, that's what I wanted for her. It was so hard letting her go. I was sad, and I hoped that this would be good for Kayla.

Kayla came to my house every other weekend. The day came when it was Kayla's ninth birthday. She was living with her daddy and she didn't come to my house on her birthday. That day I sat at my kitchen table looking out the window. I cried. I felt horrible, and I missed her so much. I wanted her back with me.

Kayla played basketball at the school she attended, the same school that I had gone to in high school. I went to see her play a couple of times. She was such a good player. She was fast, and she handled the ball very well. I loved seeing her play basketball. Her daddy had played basketball in high school, and had played the game very well, too. Kayla had gotten the talent of playing sports from her daddy.

Tara loved school, as she always had. She played the flute in the band, little league basketball, and softball. She had several good friends. Out of everything in school, the most important to Tara was making straight A's, and she did. She wanted to learn everything she could.

There were times I did get involved with Tara and Kayla's school activities. Those were the times I wasn't so depressed, and I had the energy boost that made me feel good. I felt good enough to want to do things and go places instead of staying at home in the bed. It would be great if I could just keep that energy from going away. It would come, and it would go.

Trey was quite and solemn. He was laid back, and just went with the flow. When he was around two years old, Vick taught him songs. Trey would play his little guitar and sing, *"Don't rock the juke box,"* by Alan Jackson. After he would finish singing the song, he would say, "Eat your heart out, Alan Jackson." I enjoyed Trey so much and loved seeing him grow. He was full of curiosity, and observant about everything. I was the same with Trey, though, as I was with Tara and Kayla. There were times I would laugh and play with him, and there were times when I would retire to my bedroom for a few days or weeks.

I quit my job at the cable company after I had worked there five years. It was the longest time I had ever worked at one job. At all the other jobs I had had, I did well to stay for a year. Usually, it was less than that. I needed my job to be able to help pay our bills, but that thought didn't cross my mind. I wasn't making wise decisions. I was climbing into that high of mania. I was feeling good everyday, and I was very talkative. I had energy and felt like doing things with my children. I was having a mixed episode where I went for a few days or weeks feeling really good and then the next few days or weeks, I was down and depressed. I didn't realize that this was happening. This had become my way of living. Actually, I was just existing, not living. I would swing from mania to depression.

I couldn't believe I had quit my job. I wanted to get another one. I enjoyed working, and I was much better when I worked. I could put on a different face at work. I could smile more easily when I was at work. It helped being around other people. I didn't have to dwell on being unhappy.

I began to just lie around the house most days now. I found it hard to get out of bed every morning. I didn't feel like doing anything. I didn't have much energy at all. I was beginning to get depressed to the point I felt I needed to go see a doctor about it. I had not taken any medication since I had been in the hospital about four years ago. I went to a doctor and I explained to her that I was bi-polar. I told her I was feeling depressed. We didn't have much of a discussion about it. She prescribed an anti-depressant for me, and I took them for a little while, but, just as I had done before, I didn't take them like I was supposed to. I would skip doses. I would take them every other day. Then eventually, I quit taking them at all.

We were living in Lindale, Texas, now. We had moved here when Trey was around two years old, and he was close to five years old now. There was a donut shop downtown. I saw on the window one day a sign that read "Help Wanted." I got an application, took it home, filled it out, then took it back to the donut shop.

The owner talked to me, and he hired me that day. It would be quite different than what I had done at the cable company, but I thought I would like it.

I had worked at the donut shop for about six months now. I wanted to learn how to make and cook the donuts, so the owner taught me how to do everything. It was a drive-through donut shop. I knew how to run the front window. I knew how to make and cook all the donuts we sold there. I was doing something I never thought I could do. It was a big responsibility to mix the dough, and roll it, and cut the donuts out of the dough. I made glazed, jelly filled, blueberry, chocolate, candy sprinkled and cake donuts, along with the apple fritters, and the pigs in a blanket and was ready for them to be sold by five a.m. I could do it all. I was a hard worker, and I liked my job and it was fun. I enjoyed talking to people when they drove through to get their donuts.

I was working five a.m. to twelve p.m. during the week working the drive through window. I would work from around nine p.m. to about eight a.m. on weekends preparing everything to open at five a.m. Then I cleaned the place, and by the time I went home I had flour on me from head to toe. All I was doing now was working and going home and sleeping. I wasn't focusing on my children, as I should have. I had been unhappy in my marriage for quite some time, and I began to get even more unhappy in it as time went by. I didn't want to be with Vick.

Vick and I didn't seem to see each other much. He worked during the day. I would come home, take a shower, and go to bed after I got home from work. Vick and I began to have disagreements about a lot of things. I wanted to leave. I did not want to stay with him any longer.

The troubles Vick and I had progressed, and I wanted to get out even more. One night Vick and I had a big argument, and I was planning to leave. Kayla was there, but Tara wasn't. I told Kayla we were going to leave. I picked up Trey, and Vick got furious with me about taking Trey with me. He reached out to take Trey from me. Our kitchen table got knocked over. I went to our bedroom, and Vick followed me in there. I told him I was leaving. He shoved me down on the bed and held me down with his arms, telling me I was not going to leave, and I was not going to take Trey. Our arguments had never before ended up in any kind of physical confrontation. He didn't hurt me, but I couldn't believe he had done that. I got up from our bed and went back into the living room.

I took Kayla's hand and said, "Let's go!"

"O.K., Momma let's go."

Vick was still telling me I was not going anywhere.

I said angrily to Vick, "I'll just walk to the police station." I was so angry, and I did not want to keep yelling and arguing with him. I just wanted to leave quietly with my children.

The police station was about two miles away. Kayla and I began to walk down the road quickly. We kept looking back towards our house to see if Vick was following. We were walking fast to get to the police station, and when we got there, Vick had already called them.

The police officer there told me to have a seat in his office. I sat down in a chair, and the officer talked to me. I don't know what he was saying. I was so mad, and I had just caught that he had asked me if I were taking my medication. Vick had called and told them that I was crazy and that I was bi-polar. I explained to the officer that I had not been taking my medication, but that had nothing to do with the way I was acting. I wanted to leave my house, and my husband was not letting me. I told him Vick had shoved me, knocked over our kitchen table and that he wouldn't let me take my son.

After I told him that, it was all over. It didn't seem to matter that I had left after Vick and I had argued, or that our kitchen table had gotten knocked over from all the commotion. It didn't matter that he had shoved me on the bed and held me down. It didn't matter that I did not want Kayla or Trey being there while all this was happening. I wanted to take Kayla and Trey and leave. I was angry and upset, but I was not in a state that I would have done something irrationally. Anyone who wasn't bi-polar could have acted the same way as I did in that situation.

It upset me so much that, because I had a mental illness, I was considered crazed and irrational. It didn't matter what I had to say to the police officer. It was as if the officer was not going to take me seriously because Vick had told him I was bi-polar. All I was doing was trying to prevent the arguments and take my children away from what was going on between Vick and me. I went to Teresa's house and stayed a night, then I went back home.

Kayla was with me for about a year, and then she went back to live with her daddy. Kayla seemed to be trying to figure out where her place was. When Tara and Kayla's daddy and I had divorced, Kayla took it the hardest. I know she wanted to be with her daddy and me. How was she to understand that we were not all going to be together anymore? She was only two years old then. I know it must have been very confusing to her. Tara was four when we divorced, and she dealt with things in her own way. She didn't show any signs of how it affected her, but of course, I knew it did.

Tara was twelve now and she helped me with Trey greatly. She loved her little brother. Tara took care of most of Trey's needs. She did more with Trey than I did. I didn't even realize it, but it was Tara now who took care of Trey, not me.

I couldn't bring myself to enjoy anything outside of work. I didn't do very much with my children. There were days that I felt like doing something with them, but there were more days that I didn't. I once again was not being the mother I should be. I should have been doing more things with them and spending more time with them.

I went to work one day and got angry about something at my job at the donut shop. I left the owner a note that said I was leaving, and I never went back. I had quit my job at the cable company, and now I had quit my job at the donut shop after working there for a year. I didn't know what I wanted to do. I had been up and down for a while now. I tried hard to appear happy, but I wasn't. I wanted desperately to enjoy my life.

As the years passed, I seemed to stay in a mixed episode. I didn't ever get to the point where I couldn't function, though. I left Vick two or three times, but I always went back. I continued living my life with the ups and downs of mood swings.

When Tara was fourteen years old, just before she started high school, she told me one day she wanted to live with her daddy. She wanted to go to a smaller school. By doing that, she would have a better chance of being valedictorian, which was her goal. Tara was very smart. She was mature beyond her years. School was something that she continued to make the priority of her life. But I knew there was more to Tara's leaving to go live with her dad than school. Our home life was not good with Vick and me having our problems and my being depressed so much, and I know Tara saw that.

I was losing my other daughter now. I felt I was completely to blame for my girls not wanting to live with me. I tried so hard for Tara not to see me cry. I wanted her to know that she needed to go where her heart led her. The one thing I kept in my heart was that my children would always be a part of me. They could never be taken away, even though they didn't live with me.

Not long after Tara left, I left Vick once again. I moved to a small town about fifteen miles from where we lived. I rented a very small place from a kind elderly lady. Then Kayla came back to live with me. Kayla was going back and forth between her daddy and me almost every year. I know she wanted to be with both of us. Kayla was about twelve now, and I could tell that, even after nine years, it still hurt Kayla that her daddy and momma were not together. I talked to her daddy once about having Kayla get some counseling, but it never happened.

After I moved to my new small place, I began working at a café. I was a waitress, and it wasn't a job that I liked, but I had to work. I tried to do my job well, but I had no motivation to work.

A couple of weeks or less had past when Vick moved in with me. We were back together again. This wasn't what I wanted. Kayla was with me now, but Tara was with her daddy.

I hated the fact that Tara and Kayla had been apart most of their childhood. It was bad enough that their Daddy and I had divorced, but it was worse that the girls hadn't lived together for most of the last four years.

There was a church across the street from where we were living. We began to go there. When Tara and Brittney came for the weekends, we would all go. I felt great going back to church again; church always gave me comfort. I was always delighted for my kids to be going to church, too.

The house was much too small for all of us. There was only one small bedroom, and the living room and kitchen were really small, too. There was one other small room that was only big enough for a twin bed. We could not continue to live there, so we moved yet again. This was a good move though, because the house we moved to was a much bigger house. It was spacious, with a big kitchen and living room. There were three bedrooms, so there was plenty of room for all of us.

Trey started school shortly after we moved. He was getting so big. I couldn't believe how much he had grown. It was hard for me to get excited that Trey was beginning school. I wasn't getting excited about much of anything these days. My emotions were fading away, as they had many times before.

I had quit my job at the café. I had done the same as I did at the donut shop. I got mad because my boss made a comment about the way I was making a cake, so I walked out the back door without telling anyone I was leaving, and I didn't go back.

I was staying at home now. I just got more depressed. I had to get a job. I had to go to work. We needed the money. I had been spending my days in the bed almost all day. I didn't care what I looked like. There were a lot of days I didn't get dressed until late afternoon, right before Trey got home from school and Vick got home from work.

I applied for a job at the elementary school in the town I lived in now. I again got the job and started working in the school cafeteria, and as a school bus monitor when school let out. But I didn't stay at that job for very long, either. It was so hard at this time to make myself go to work. I didn't have the energy or the desire to get out of the house. I stayed home again and continued being depressed.

After a few months, I began looking for another job. I applied for a job at a grocery store, and a few days later I got a phone call from the manager telling me I had gotten the job. I started working there, but I had to force myself to go everyday. Working didn't help like it had in the past. I wasn't able to hide my depression when I went to work. I didn't talk to anyone at my job. I wanted to leave as soon as I got there. I just couldn't put any effort into doing my job well. On my way to work, I dreaded going to this job more than any job I had ever had. I worked a lot of evenings and weekends, and I hated that.

Kayla had gone to the new school where we had lived now for just a short time, and then she moved back in with her daddy. When Tara and Kayla were at the house on the weekends they came to stay with me, I didn't have much time with them because I was working. I found it hard when they did come to get up out of bed and enjoy them, even if I didn't have to go to work. I had to force myself to get out of bed. I didn't have much of an appetite anymore. I weighed about one hundred twenty pounds, but I had begun to lose weight.

I quit my job at the grocery store after a couple of months. Most of my previous jobs had helped me to feel good about myself. This one, though, I just could not do this time. It was close to Christmas, and I was told I had to work Christmas Eve. I was not going to do that, so I told my manager I was working too many nights, and I couldn't work Christmas Eve. Then I left. Once again, I quit a job knowing I had to work because we needed the money to pay our bills. I was not being able to hold a job.

I wanted to leave Vick once again. There had been too many things happen in our marriage that were not good. We had separated a few times, but it was never for very long at a time. I had come to realize I could not and did not want to stay in this marriage any longer. The best thing that had come from it was having my son, Trey.

I had stayed in a marriage that I was unhappy in for years. I left Vick, and Trey and I went to live with Mother, as I had done so many times. I always went back to Mother's or one of my sister's houses when I was in need and could not make it on my own—every time I was depressed and couldn't see how I could live on my own. I didn't know how I could afford it, but also I couldn't stand the fact of having to be alone. I didn't have a job. I would have to start all over again as I had done several times before in the past.

Since I had become an adult, I began to realize that Mother had always taken care of me. That's how she had shown her love to me all my life. As a child, I wanted attention and affection from her. My adulthood was a roller coaster of living depressed or in mania. So many times I went through depression, Mother took me in her home and didn't think twice about how many times she had done that. When I was in that hospital during my severe manic episode for three months, she gave all she had to make sure her daughter would be happy again. Even though she hadn't told me the words, "I love you," or had given me the hugs that I so longed for as a child, she gave me her ultimate attention by being the person who was always there beside me. She gave me more comfort and encouragement now than she did when I was child. It proved Mother's unconditional love for me. I had always seen her strength, and now her strength is what I longed for. I wanted to be strong enough to live life relying on myself and knowing I could make it on my own. Mother never once let me down in my time of need.

Going through my divorce with Vick brought me way down. I had been depressed for quite some time now and was gradually getting worse. I could not get out of it. I wanted so desperately to feel better and enjoy life.

I looked in the help wanted ads in the newspaper and went and applied for a job that I found in the paper. I was hired and began working at an office supply company in the printing department. I was doing better at this job. I liked this job and the people I worked with. Again, as I had done at other jobs, I was able to put on a different face and hide my depression, although, I was rather quite there. I went to work and then went home and stayed there every evening. I didn't go anywhere else but to work. On the weekends, I didn't do anything, either. I just didn't feel like going anywhere. I had no desire to have a social life.

Kayla was still with her dad, and Tara was also there. I missed my girls so much. I did have Trey with me, and I was tremendously thankful for that. Trey was keeping me going. I wanted to be a happy momma for Trey, and I tried, but I couldn't get past the sadness of what my life had become. I did feel some better after I left Vick.

I went to work during the day, and Trey went to school. Trey was six years old now. Trey would ride the school bus to Mother's after school and was there when I got home from work. We would all sit down and eat supper together. Afterwards, we watched TV. I didn't really pay attention to the TV, though, because I couldn't focus on it and had no desire to.

In the evenings, Trey would ask me to play Pac-Man with him. He wanted me to go outside with him to play. I had not gotten completely past the depression I had been in, and some days it was difficult for me to do things even with Trey. However, I made myself take time with Trey and do the things he wanted me to do with him. I realized he needed attention from me.

This was all hard for Trey, too. His momma and daddy were not together anymore. Trey didn't cry or question why we weren't all together any more. He continued to go with the flow and be as happy-go-lucky as he had always been. He needed me as much as I needed him. Having him with me helped me to get through my days. I began to get less depressed.

It had been two or three months now from the time I had left Vick. He began to ask me if Trey could come live with him. I told him no each time. I wanted Trey to be with me. I would not let him go. Vick didn't give up on it, though. He told me a boy needs to be with his daddy. I continued telling Vick Trey was going to stay with me. I was not giving in to letting Trey go live with him. I just couldn't do that. Trey was the only child I had with me now. I could not lose him. I loved Trey with all my heart. Vick saw that I was not going to agree to have Trey live with him. He told me he would take Trey, and I would not see him. He told me he would tell the court that I was crazy, and that they would believe him. Would he really do those things? I believed that he would. I didn't seem to have a choice now. I could not go to court because I felt I could not win against Vick telling them I was bi-polar. I was convinced that's what would happen. I felt I was a good momma and I loved my children, yet again I was a failure at being a mother. I let Trey go live with him. I couldn't take the chance of not seeing Trey. If I let Trey go to live with Vick, I knew I would be able to see him at least every other weekend. All three of my children were not with me now. I felt horrible for letting Trey go. What had I done? Why didn't I fight to keep my son? I was furious with Vick for telling me the things he did. I believed he knew he would scare me when he told me the court would believe

I was crazy. I didn't want to be perceived as crazy. No matter how hard I tried to be a good mother, it just didn't seem to be good enough to have my children. I would regret for the rest of my life that I had not gone to court and proved I was a good mother, and was capable of taking care of my son even though I was bi-polar. I was broken hearted when Trey went to live with his daddy.

I never told people I was bi-polar. People would definitely treat me differently if I told them. Still, after eight years of being diagnosed as bi-polar, people did not utter a word about it. The stigmatism of it made me afraid to tell anyone. I knew people would not understand what it truly was; it would only be that I was crazy, weird and strange. The only people that knew were my family and the people that knew me at the church I had gone to since I was a baby. There were people in Alba, Texas where I had lived when I was married to Tara and Kayla's daddy that knew, but they were no longer in my life.

Tracy and Delaine, my friends I had gone to high school with in Alba knew. They had seen what I went through with my depression when I was twenty-two. They had come to see me when I was in the hospital ten years ago. They knew I wasn't crazy. They accepted me because they saw me as the person I truly was.

Tracy and I kept in touch through the years. I never wanted to lose touch with her. She knew me so well, and she came to be the friend in my life who I knew would always be there for me in any situation. She knew the person I was before I ever knew I was bi-polar. She never gave up hope on my getting better. We had great conversations and she could always make me laugh. We had talked about the days when I went through those episodes. Tracy told me that, during those times, she knew I was in there somewhere, and she believed I would get better and be the person she knew again. I have not met another person who could ever be what Tracy was to me. She was my friend whom I will always be grateful to have. She always knew just the right thing to say to me in all situations. She understood me. I will cherish our friendship forever.

I applied for a job where Teresa was working and was hired. It would be a job where I would make more money. My boss at the office supply company wanted me to stay: he told me he liked the work I did for him. I was surprised. I had put all I had into being a good employee there, and now I knew I had. I had been depressed when I began working there, but I had been able to do my job well. Going back to work did help me to feel much less depressed. I had to move on for better money, though, and the new job would be something that I felt I would enjoy more. I went to work at a medical office with several doctors that were ophthalmologist. I checked out patients and did insurance referrals for the patients. I was enjoying my new job, and feeling even better now. I was around more people. Everybody was kind to me, and I was able to talk to all of them. I was always so quite at the job I had left. I really enjoyed the conversation with the people I worked with now. I loved talking to the patients. It had been a while since I had talked to people so freely.

I began to talk about my children to my co-workers. I knew the questions would come, though. The questions that would lead them to know my children did not live with me. I didn't want to tell people my girls lived with their daddy, and my son lived with his daddy, too. I just knew they would judge me. I knew they would wonder why I didn't have my children. I was afraid they would think I was a horrible mother. I knew they would think I must have done something wrong or bad since my children weren't with me. I wanted people to know how much I loved my children, and I wanted everyone to know I didn't abandon them. I didn't like to talk to people about it, although I wanted everyone to know all about them and how they were the most important people in my life.

I knew my children loved me and that they knew I loved them. I had been depressed so often as Tara and Kayla were growing up. I had stayed in bed and slept so much of my life. They had a momma who was sad and miserable. Tara and Kayla had a momma who was sick, and I still did not know that bi-polar had been in control of me ever since they were little girls. Trey was seven now, and he was seeing me behave the same way.

I met a lady, Patty, at my new job, and we began to talk to each other a lot. She and Teresa had known each other for quite a few years. We became friends and began to do things together. I was feeling much better about myself, and I felt my job performance was appreciated. I was doing well at my job. My spirits were high. I had much more energy than I had had for the past several months.

I moved from Mother's, and I moved in with Patty. Patty helped me greatly. When I was down, she would pick me up. She would talk to me with encouraging words. I had not had a friend like her whom I could confide in for a long time. I told her all about Tara, Kayla, and Trey. I talked to her about things that I couldn't talk about to other people. I told her so much of my life. She would listen to me, and she told me things that made me feel like I was a good person. I needed a friend like Patty now in my life, and, thank God, I had one.

It had been at least a year now since I had left Vick. We had filed for a divorce several months back. He told me he would go to court, and that I didn't need to since it would be just to sign papers and then it would be over. I signed the paper giving my consent for the divorce so that he could take it to court with him. He had also told me he didn't want any child support from me whatsoever and that he was not going to ask for any. Just a few days after he went to court, I received papers saying I would have to pay child support. Again, I had believed what Vick had told me. I didn't know what I was going to do now. I didn't have enough money to live on my own, and now I would have even less.

There was very little communication between Tara and Kayla's daddy and me. We had no problems with each other. For the most part, we agreed on things when it came to our girls.

On the other hand, I didn't want to talk to Vick at all. Our conversations in person, or over the telephone, always ended up in an argument. He called me at home and at work a lot, for unnecessary reasons. I wanted him to just leave me alone, but he wouldn't. We had parted ways in an ugly manner.

I often wondered if Trey thought I didn't want him to live with me. He was seven years old, and I was afraid Trey would wonder why he wasn't with his momma. I wanted him to know how much I loved him, and that I wanted him to be with me always.

Patty and I started going out places and it helped to get out of the house. I met a man, whose name was Todd, one night at a place where Patty and I went. I was attracted to him the first time I met him. He called me and asked if I wanted to go out with him. Of course I did; I was excited to have met him. We were together as much as we could be after that night. I enjoyed being with him, and we had fun together. He was very polite to me, and he made me feel special. I actually had a boyfriend now, and I was much happier than I had been in months. I could not believe how much better life had finally become.

I was thirty-six years old now. Tara was sixteen, and Kayla was fourteen. They had moved with their daddy to Albuquerque, New Mexico, almost a year ago. I was missing out on their teenage years. We wrote letters to each other. They would tell me what they were doing in school and all about their friends they had met. I was delighted to get each letter they sent. I would read them over and over again. I was sad that they were living there. Again, I just wanted them to be happy wherever they decided to be. That was what was most important to me.

Tara and Kayla came to see me during their spring break. I was thrilled, and overjoyed to see them. I was finally able to spend time with them. We talked and laughed, and I enjoyed them being with me after all this time. When the week was over, Tara went back to her daddy's, but Kayla decided to stay with me. I was excited and happy that Kayla was going to live with me again, but I was scared, also. I was still living with Patty, and I didn't have much money. I wouldn't be able to get a place of our own for Kayla and me to live. I was afraid I wouldn't have the money to get Kayla the things she wanted, much less what she needed. I wanted to be able to provide for her in every way.

A few weeks passed, and Kayla and I went to live with my sister, Debbie. I thought being there would be better for us. Once again, I had gone to live with one of my sisters. We didn't stay with Debbie and her family for very long, however. Kayla and I moved in with my boyfriend, Todd. Kayla liked him, which made it all good. I was falling in love with him. He was a hard worker and a responsible man who was there for me in every way.

His mobile home he had was spacious, and I loved it. Kayla had her own room with a nice bedroom suit that was Todd's. She had her own bathroom. Todd and I wanted her to be comfortable there. He bought her a stereo to have in her room. Of course, I wanted everything to be pleasant for Kayla.

Kayla started again in a new school. She had gone to so many different schools throughout her life, and that bothered me. She made new friends and got involved in sports, which was something she was very good at and loved. She seemed to make the adjustment of moving here with no problem. Kayla was always free-spirited. Everyone she met liked her, so it was easy for her to make friends, with her fun and loving personality. It was so great to have her home with me again.

I enjoyed being with Todd and thought our relationship would be long term. Kayla was with me now, and Trey came to see me every other weekend and one evening every other week. Tara lived too far away to visit often, but she was with me in my heart. I was with a man who treated me with respect and kindness. My children liked him, and he was as good to them as he was to me. He accepted my children, and I appreciated that. My life had totally changed in the past year. I could see that Todd felt deeply for me, as I did him. Happiness had come my way.

I was no longer depressed, and I had lots of energy these days. Then my energy began to escalate more and more. I began to stay up late almost every night and got up very early each morning to go to work. Then I began to stay up all night, many nights at a time. I would wash clothes, fold them, and put them away neatly in their places. I would listen to music and sometimes would dance around in the living room at night after Kayla went to bed. I was enjoying having all this energy. I felt good everyday. I didn't feel tired or feel the need to sleep. I went to work every day, even though I slept very little or, some nights, none at all. With all the energy I had, staying up at night with little to no sleep didn't affect my being able to go to work. Todd worked nights, and he didn't realize that I was not sleeping at night.

We were clearing off Todd's land he had his mobile home on. Trees had been cut down, and we had piles of brush that we were going to burn. I would go outside almost every night and burn the piles of brush. I would be outside burning them for hours. While they were burning, I would keep my car doors open and listen to the radio blaring from my car.

One night, I was burning outside, and Kayla came outside and found me lying on the ground by the fire. I'm sure I had fallen asleep by a burn pile from pure exhaustion. Kayla picked me up and carried me into the house. Later, she told me that she had done that, but I didn't really give it much thought. I didn't realize that Kayla had had to make sure that the fire did not harm me.

The thoughts I was having now were about things that weren't real. When I took a bath at night, I thought there was always someone outside the window above the bathtub. I would think that there were two or three men outside. I wasn't scared of them, though. They couldn't see me, and I couldn't see them. They just stood outside by the window while I bathed. I felt that they were protecting me.

While I ran my bath water, I would place my shoulders and arms under very hot water. I thought the hot water would turn my skin red like a sunburn. This would cause my skin to be tanned. I wanted my fair skin to be brown.

My sex drive had been becoming more intense for a while. I wanted sex a lot now. It was something I wanted more and more of. Sex was something I craved, just as it had been with Vick years ago.

There was a very small wood-frame house behind the mobile home where we lived. I believed that Alan Jackson, the country music singer, lived there. I never saw him coming or going from the house, but I just knew he lived there. The only time I thought about him living there was when I was outside burning the brush piles late at night. I would look at the house and wonder if he was looking out the window at me. I listened to the music blaring from my car so he would know I listened to country music. He was one of my favorite country music singers.

There were too many strange thoughts that were in my head. My mind was playing tricks on me again. I had no doubt all these delusions I was having were completely true and real, but they weren't.

Kayla was watching her mother becoming a person she couldn't understand. She took it upon herself to take care of me. She watched out for me. She didn't know what was wrong with me, but she had to have known something was. She didn't tell anyone about all the things she was seeing me do that were out of the ordinary. She wanted to believe that nothing was wrong with me and that I was okay. She would not believe any differently.

Tara came to stay with me during her spring break as she did last year. She was growing up so much and was so beautiful. I was missing out on all her teenage years. It almost felt as if she came and left in the same day. When she left, I didn't remember sitting down talking to her or doing anything with her. I remembered seeing her there, and then she was gone. I didn't know it, but Tara felt that I was sick again. She had come to recognize the signs.

Most of the bizarre thoughts I had came at night. I functioned fine during the day, as far as I knew. My problem during the day was the high energy I had. This energy continued all day and all night. I felt great. I didn't realize that as my depression went away, I was slowly getting manic again.

I wasn't able to focus on my job much anymore. It was hard for me to sit still in my chair at work. I would take smoke breaks more than I was supposed to. I was frustrated because I wasn't able to focus on what I was supposed to be doing. I was telling my co-workers I had too much work and that I needed someone to help me with my job. I just got worse and worse at not being able to do my job duties. Actually, my job wasn't to stressful; it was just that I couldn't handle it anymore. My brain was going much faster with racing thoughts as time passed. I couldn't keep up with it. I couldn't finish something before I would start doing something else. I was going into the extreme highs of mania now.

I was at work one day, and it hit me all of a sudden. Something was not right. There was something wrong with me again. It worried me because I didn't know exactly what was happening, but I knew something needed to be done. I thought back to the last manic episode I had when I was in the hospital for three months. I did not want that to happen again. I found a phone book at work, and I started thumbing through the yellow pages looking for a psychiatrist to call. I didn't know why I was making this phone call. I hadn't seen a psychiatrist in about ten years now. I hadn't thought about needing to go see one until this very day. I called the first one listed under "psychiatrist." I hadn't thought anything was wrong with me until just this very moment. I called the first doctor listed in the yellow pages, and I made an appointment to go see Dr. Joseph P. Arisco. I wrote down the date and time of my appointment, and then I didn't think about it again.

I found another job because I was tired of not being able to do the job I had, but I couldn't do it because they wouldn't let anyone help me. It wasn't because anything was wrong with me, I thought. Up until now, I had loved my job and had no problem doing it.

I gave my two-week notice. I thought I was making a good decision, although, I would be making three dollars less an hour than what I made at the job I was leaving. I thought the new job would be less stressful, and that's what I needed. What was I thinking? I wasn't thinking. When I talked to Todd about it, he asked me how much I would be making. I avoided telling him because I knew now this was not a wise decision. I had not thought out this important decision at all. I had just acted out of impulse.

My new job was working at a car dealership. I worked in a building across from the main dealership where they sold vehicles. The building in which I worked was where the dealership kept their eighteen-wheeler trucks. I went to orientation a couple of days after I started my job in the main building of the car dealership.

After the orientation, someone was to give me a ride in one of the eighteen-wheelers. I barreled out of the main building when orientation was over. I ran across Loop 323, which is a six-lane highway, and then across Hwy 69, which was a four-lane highway, to get to the building where I worked. I was running as fast as I could. I wasn't even thinking of the cars that were passing by. Why the hell did I take off running into the highway? All I could think of is getting my ride in one of the eighteen-wheelers.

I waited outside the building for a man who was to take me for my ride. No one ever came to take me on that ride. Where was he? When was he coming to take me for my ride? I got so mad that I got in my car and left my job. I don't know how long I drove around. I didn't know where I was going. In fact, I didn't need to be going anywhere. After all, I was supposed to be at work.

While I was driving, I wasn't thinking about how mad I was anymore. It was as if I were going somewhere I needed to go. I wasn't thinking that I had just left my job because someone didn't give me a ride in a truck. Then I realized, oh my gosh, I had left work. I've got to go back. I knew as I was driving back to work that I would not have that job anymore.

I got back to my job, and I went straight to my boss. I told him I knew I had lost my job. I had told him that my other job was too stressful when he had asked me why I wanted this job during my interview with him. He told me he didn't think this would be a stressful job, and I told him that wasn't it, but that I was having some other problems. I didn't know what else to tell him. I felt awful. This man had given me a job, and this is what I had done to him. At that moment, I realized I did have a problem. Something was wrong with me. Most of the time, I didn't think that what I was doing or thinking was unusual. I knew now I did need to get some help.

No one had ever told me someone was going to take me on a ride in one of those eighteen-wheelers. That was never meant to happen. Why I thought it was, I don't know. What a crazy thing to think. I had truly believed it was going to happen.

When I was severely depressed in 1982, it was all about being a bad mother. When I had been depressed in 1989 after divorcing Tara and Kayla's daddy it had turned to severe mania. Then, it was all about protecting my kids from everyone. Now it was 1998, and again I had gotten depressed. I went through another failed marriage. My children did not live with me after I had divorced Vick. I had been so sad and miserable before, and after my divorce from him. Then when Trey went to live with him, I was devastated. I had felt that I would never have my children with me again.

Then six months after that, Kayla came back to live with me. I enjoyed having all the time I had with Trey. I was with a man whom I loved, and my life had become so much better. This time, as before, my depression had preceded the severe mania that had come again.

Through the years of my early thirties I lived with highs and lows. I was in my late thirties and I still would not admit I had a problem with depression. I took medication, for depression off and on through my thirties, but not very often, and I never took it the way it was prescribed. I would take it for a week or two. I would skip doses. If I didn't have the money to get it, I didn't worry about it. I would take one every other day, thinking that would be sufficient until I was able to buy another prescription. Sometimes, not having the money was an excuse because I would think I might need that money for something else; I would wait for the medication. I didn't know yet how important it was to take my medication and that I would do better when I took it the right way.

I never, ever, took my depression or the highs and lows seriously. I didn't think it was serious. I just denied my mental illness. How could I have been diagnosed with bi-polar? How could those doctors know that? It had to be something else. I didn't know what it was, but I was not crazy. What would people think of me if they knew I was bi-polar? At the time, it still was not something people knew a lot about or talked about. I refused to believe I was bi-polar, and I certainly did not want anyone else to know I was.

This was my life; living this way was all I really knew. Why should my life be different if I took medication? I didn't believe it could be. I had no idea. I didn't know my life could have been better; it was normal to me.

All through the years, my late twenties through my mid thirties, were lost years for me. I missed out on so much of my children's lives throughout these years. I wasn't living my life to the fullest. I was depressed so much of the time. I had manic episodes at times, too, but for the most, depression came my way more than mania did.

TREATMENT AGAIN

I remembered I had made an appointment to see the psychiatrist. The day came when I was to go for my appointment. When I got there, I had to fill out papers with all the same questions, just as I had done when I went to see my first psychiatrist. I don't know how much of them I answered, or if I answered any of them. I don't know why I had come here, nor did I know why I had made the appointment. Since making the appointment, I began thinking again that nothing was wrong with me.

My name was called, and I followed the doctor into his office. I began to tell this doctor nothing was wrong with me. I told him I didn't need medication, and I told him these things very firmly. I didn't give the doctor a chance to tell me how he could help me. If he did tell me, I didn't pay any attention to him. Then I walked out of his office, got in my car, and left. I knew something was wrong, but, on the other hand, I believed I was fine. I battled with myself over whether I really needed help or not. I wanted so desperately not to be sick again. I wanted to believe I was all right, but, on the other hand, I knew I could end up the way I had been ten years ago.

After I left his office, I didn't even remember driving there. I didn't remember filling out any papers. I didn't remember the doctor saying anything at all to me. I didn't remember where I went after I left his office. The whole appointment was like a blur to me. My mind had gone blank.

One night at home while I was taking a bath, I started splashing water everywhere and acting very strange. Todd was there, and he called Debbie and told her something was wrong with me and he didn't know what to do. Debbie and Teresa came over and sat all night with me. That was when they realized I was definitely in another episode of mania.

When I went to see Dr. Arisco, I acted as if there was no reason for me to be there. Why would he want me as a patient? I had not listened to anything he had said to me. How could this doctor help me if I was not going to accept that anything was wrong? What good would it do? I desperately needed help now. I was not able to comprehend in my head that I was in a manic episode again.

I wasn't aware of it, but Debbie called Dr. Arisco to talk to him about me. When Debbie called him, he told her how I acted on the day I went to see him. He told her I had been this way all my life. Debbie assured him I had not. But, in fact, I had lived my life with bi-polar for many years. Dr. Arisco refused to see me as a patient, but Debbie pleaded with him to see me. She knew I desperately needed help. After her pleas, Dr. Arisco did agree to see me as his patient. My family was very supportive, and, again, they were going to do all they could to help me become stable. I believe Dr. Arisco saw that my family was willing to help me, and I definitely needed them in order to get better.

Soon after the scene in the bathtub, Todd and a friend of his took me to a place to get treatment. I had no idea where I was being taken or even that I was going to get treatment. If they had told me, I didn't remember it. Debbie and Teresa thought I would really be upset and would possibly get out of control when I got there and realized where I was. When we did get there, it was the same hospital I had gone to ten years ago, where I stayed for three months. However, I was calm, and I didn't have any problem being there. Debbie and Teresa had met us there; we walked in, and I was checked in. I didn't have any idea that this was the same place I had been in all those years ago. One thing that had changed here, was the name of the hospital.

I checked in as an out-patient instead of an in-patient this time. Dr. Arisco told my family that he did not think it would be a good idea that I be hospitalized again. Not after what had happened to me before. Dr. Arisco had actually been affiliated with the hospital when I had been there before during my last manic episode. Neither my family nor I knew this.

Out-patient, in-patient; it didn't mean anything to me. I didn't know I had come back to the same place that had been pure hell for me. I didn't realize I was going to be treated for bi-polar disorder. I just went along with it all, not knowing what was going on.

Part of my treatment consisted of going to group sessions. The other people who were coming here filled the session room. The room was narrow and long, with chairs lined up along the walls. At the front of the room was a chalkboard. Also, at the front of the room, the teacher, speaker, counselor, or whatever she was stood in front of the chalkboard. I had been through all this before. Last time it hadn't made a difference. Would it this time?

Debbie or Teresa would take me to the behavior health facility for my treatment every day. There were times when my niece, Nicole, and Kayla would come pick me up instead of my sisters. Once again, my family set their lives aside to take care of me. I wasn't able to drive anymore; it wasn't safe. I was totally out of reality now, living beyond reality again.

When I went through the front door of the facility, I would go through a door to the left that led into a big room. There were chairs and couches to sit in. At the end of the big open area there was a smaller area that was a mini-kitchen, with a sink and a refrigerator. There were drinks and snacks available there for the patients. To the right of the open area were a few small rooms where a patient went to have a visit with his or her doctor. I would see three doctors when I was there: Dr. Arisco and two other ones. I knew the other two were doctors because people went into one of the small rooms with them, just as I did with Dr. Arisco. There was one other small room with a plastic window all around it and a door to go into it. There was always a young man there shuffling papers. I never could figure out why he was there.

They would let us take short breaks during the group session. We would go outside to an area where there were plants and small trees, and iron chairs and benches to sit in. It was a pleasant, fenced-in area, bigger than the patio area where I went out when I was hospitalized here. I would stand with the other patients outside and smoke. We would gather and talk, and at times I joined the conversations they were having. Sometimes, I would sit in one of the patio chairs alone with my own thoughts.

I never realized this place I was coming to now was the same place I had been kept for three long months before. It didn't look familiar. I had not seen this area when I was here before. Just as before, I would go out when I was told I could, and I would go back in when someone came to get me.

Nothing mattered to me anymore. I was doing a lot of the same things I had done before. I could not be by myself. I was in my own world again, with time meaning nothing, bizarre thoughts in my head, behavior that was out of the ordinary, and my belief that nothing was wrong with me. All of these things were back. I didn't know it, but my family did.

I was living with Mother again. I couldn't live with my boyfriend, Todd, any longer. I had told him I was bi-polar not long after we starting seeing each other. I told him some of the things that had happened to me, and some of the things I had done when I had been manic before. There was just no way he could ever understand the whole concept of it. It was hard for anyone to understand. I couldn't say enough to him to let him know what it was all about. I knew, though, that I shouldn't and couldn't keep it from him. It would be wrong for me not to tell him. What would happen if I were to become severely depressed or manic again? He wouldn't know what to do, or what was happening to me. The sad thing was, it did happen, and, just as I had thought, he didn't know what to think or do for me.

I had started into a manic episode before I moved in with Todd, just as I had done before I had met Vick. Throughout that marriage, I had become unhappy and depressed much of the time. I had stayed in a mixed episode with the ups of mania and the downs of depression since I had met Vick. After a time, I knew that being bi-polar had affected my marriage with Tara and Kayla's daddy in some ways, also. I had two failed marriages, and now the relationship I was in had also ended in failure.

My energy level was still extremely high. It was hard for Mother to take care of me alone. She had to watch just about my every move. She never knew what I would do. I might run out the door and run down the road. I might go in a room and just ransack the whole place. I would try to iron my clothes when I really didn't have a clue about being careful with the iron. I could have easily burned myself. There were so many other things I was doing, and I didn't even know I was doing them. The thoughts were racing in my head again, and I could not get them to leave or slow down. I hardly knew what I was doing from one minute to the next. I wasn't able to sleep for any length of time.

There was one day when I was at Mother's and I went outside and ran down the dead end road Mother lived on. I ran to the end of the road and went up to the last house. I went up to a window and cupped my hands around my eyes and looked in. The furniture I saw was so pretty. Everything in this house looked beautiful. I wanted to go in. I wanted this house to be my house. It looked so comfortable and cozy. Then, I ran back to Mother's house and she was standing on the front porch calling for me.

In my room at Mother's house, I started piling my clothes all over the room once again, as I had done during my last manic episode. In fact, I was just making a huge mess. In my mind, I was organizing them, putting the shirts with the pants I would wear with them, and putting the same color of clothes together. I would have three or four piles scattered all over the room. I would fold them, and fold them again, or just lay them on top of each other without folding them. I couldn't think logically anymore. I couldn't seem to get my thoughts in perspective to think logically.

I began to stay with Debbie or Teresa mostly now, instead of Mother. I would stay at Debbie's house for a day or two, then I would go to Teresa's for a day or so. It was too difficult for only one of them to have me stay with them every day. Debbie and Teresa had to go to work, and they had to take care of their families. Their lives revolved around making sure I was not going to do anything irrationally. I know it was very exhausting for them. If I wasn't sleeping, they couldn't sleep. If I went outside, they had to go outside, too. It took both of them to care for me. They had to put their lives on the back burner to take care of me. They had to watch me as if I were a child. They had to make sure I didn't go through their house destroying it. I would drag things out of the refrigerator; I would go and ransack rooms in their houses: I would try to go outside and walk or run off.

I didn't care much for going to my sessions at the behavioral health facility. I would sit in a chair and half-way listen to the person at the front of the room. I would watch everyone else in the room. We were often given papers with questions to answer. Some of the people would talk, but I never said much at all. I didn't know how this was supposed to help me. Most of the time, the subject was about being an alcoholic or a drug addict. I didn't have those problems. The papers that was handed out to us to read and answer questions from meant nothing to me.

Debbie or Teresa would take me there and go inside with me; then they went to work. I stayed in the open area until I was told to go into the session room. I would go in one of the offices and talk with Dr. Arisco if he was there. I had come to like Dr. Arisco a lot and was glad when I had a visit with him. I would listen to what he told me. Out of all the doctors, I thought Dr. Arisco was the best. I didn't know anything about the other doctors, but I knew my doctor was the best one.

I went to the sessions at the behavior health center for a couple of weeks. Then one day I was there and decided I wasn't going to come there anymore. I went into the small office where the young man was always sitting, shuffling papers. This was the office that had the plastic window all around it. I told the man I wanted to check out and that I did not need to come here anymore. Actually, what happened was, I no longer could go there because I was just to manic. I wasn't able to sit still long enough while I was there, so I was released. The behavioral health center could not give me the treatment I needed because my mania was so severe.

I continued going to see Dr. Arisco at the office where he had his practice. I was taking the medication I was prescribed. I had been prescribed lithium and some other medications. I took two lithium in the morning and two at night. A sleeping pill had been prescribed to help me sleep, but it didn't make me sleep for very long at a time. I would sleep maybe two or three hours after I took it, and then I was awake again. I did not have to take anywhere near the amount of medication I had been given during my last episode, though.

Debbie took me to my friend Patty's house one day. I wanted to see her. After all, we had been roommates before all this had happened to me, and we had been close friends for a year or more. When Debbie came to pick me up, Teresa came also. I didn't want to leave Patty's; I wanted to stay the night there. Patty told Debbie it would be fine for me to stay, but Debbie would not allow it. I started yelling at Debbie, telling her I was going to stay. Debbie and I argued until it got pretty intense. I was furious. Why couldn't I stay just one night here? I couldn't do anything! I was tired of everybody telling me I couldn't do this or that. I had never had a real confrontation with Debbie or Teresa. We never argued. We had always gotten along very well, and we were all very close to each other. Since I had been in this episode, though, I had argued and yelled at them often. Kayla was there at Patty's, too. That night was horrible and sad. Debbie and Teresa told Kayla and me that Kayla was going to have to go back to her daddy's.

"No!" I yelled at Debbie.

I did not want Kayla to leave and go back to her daddy's, and Kayla didn't either. Kayla was crying, and there was more yelling. We were all standing outside at Patty's house, and Kayla was saying she was not leaving. It seemed to break Kayla's heart knowing that she would have to leave me, but it was best for her to go back to her daddy's. I was not taking care of Kayla like I should have been, I couldn't, in the shape I was in. She was not getting what she needed from me as her mother. She really didn't need to watch what was happening with me. She had seen enough, all ready; actually too much. She was only fourteen. She did not need to feel that she was responsible for taking care of me.

I didn't think about what Kayla or Trey thought about all this. Tara was still living with her daddy. I didn't realize what Kayla and Trey were seeing happen to me. They didn't know what was wrong with me, and I'm sure they could not understand it. It never crossed my mind how difficult it was for them to see me acting so strangely. I didn't wonder what any of my family thought, though. After all, I still did not believe anything was wrong with me. I thought I was fine.

My behavior was getting more and more bizarre. I was doing even more strange things now. I didn't realize what I was doing, and I thought that all my behavior was normal. In fact, it wasn't. It was very much out of the ordinary and far from normal.

There was a pair of men's shoes at Mother's, and I thought they were Dr. Arisco's. I'd put them outside on the porch, and then I would bring them back inside and place them right by the front door and leave them there. Then I would go on to something else and forget about them. When I noticed them again, I would move them. One time his shoes were outside when it had rained, and the shoes had gotten wet. Now, I'd have to get them dry, so I took them in the house. The rain had stopped and the sun was shining. I sat the shoes back on the porch in the sun to dry. His shoes stayed either on the porch outside or right inside the house near the front door. With those shoes being there, it was as if Dr. Arisco were here. I didn't tell anyone they were Dr. Arisco's shoes. Again, I didn't tell any of my thoughts to anyone; I kept them all inside my head.

I went to Teresa's when it was her turn to take care of me. When at her house, I would stay in my niece Nicole's room. I would go through all her clothes and shoes, which I could wear. I weighed around one hundred pounds now. I would put her clothes on and then I would take them off, over and over, like I was a child playing dress up. One day I was in her room, and I destroyed it. I threw her things all over her room and made a complete mess of it. I went through it like a tornado. I took the mums she had hanging on her wall that she had gotten for special occasions in school and threw them on the floor. I took all her nick knacks off her dresser. I ransacked her closet. Teresa was furious with me. She couldn't make me understand that I shouldn't do that sort of thing.

Nicole's friends would come over sometimes. Nicole was seventeen at the time, and she and her friends were in high school. I had no idea what her friends thought of me. I didn't know what Nicole had told them about me. They probably thought I was odd, and, probably, crazy, because I acted really strange. Nicole had two or three of her friends at the apartment one day. They went outside and sat on the steps in front of Teresa's apartment. I went outside and sat on the steps with them, and I acted just like them, like a teenager. I was acting silly, talking to them, and we were laughing. I probably was the one causing all the laughing. The way I was acting was probably ridiculous to them.

Teresa kept coming outside checking on me. If it looked like I might walk off, she would say, "Get back up here; you can't go over there."

She would come out time after time. I would walk a few paces away from the steps, and she would say again, "Get back up here!"

I would get angry with her and yell, "I'm not going anywhere!"

I asked her, "Why can't I go over there?"

She would tell me, "You just can't." Just like you would tell a child.

I couldn't do anything. Someone was always telling me "No, you can't do that," or "No, you can't go there."

My thoughts were about all sorts of things. I did think about running away, far, far, away. I could go anywhere I wanted to go. I didn't need anybody. There were no thoughts that I would be alone. It wouldn't be scary to me; I didn't think about it being dangerous. I didn't think about where I would live. I could run away, and everyone would leave me alone.

I talked to people like they were right beside me, but, in reality, no one was there. I didn't realize I was doing that, nor did I realize a lot of the things I was doing. I lived in my private world with my strange thoughts and my bizarre behavior.

I began to wear all black clothes before I had stopped going to my out-patient treatment, but I didn't notice that I was. My family was told to watch me carefully. Wearing black could be a sign that I was suicidal. During this time, I wasn't sad. I thought I was acting just as normal as every one else. I would get angry, but my anger never turned violent though. Although, I would throw temper-tantrums as a child would. I never felt like I wanted to die. Thoughts of suicide did not enter my mind.

I went to Debbie's when it was her turn to keep me. I didn't ever remember being there. I know it was a huge chore for her, too, though, when I was at her house. Debbie finally could not handle my being at her house as often any more. She knew she was on the verge of falling apart. She had to think of herself, and her family. The worry and stress was a tremendous strain on my sisters, but they still never gave up hope that the day would come when I would be better.

I was staying at Mother's during the day now, since I was no longer going to my out-patient treatment. I would stay the nights with Teresa. I still stayed with Debbie some, but not as much as I was with Teresa. They all had to have some relief from me, so they could rest and get some sleep. Teresa and Debbie both had their jobs they had to go to. Mother and my sisters must have been completely exhausted, but they didn't give up on me.

My second cousin, Charles would come to Mother's to see us. Mother was sixty-three years old now, and Charles had gone to school with Mother and Daddy. He was very nice to me, and he was funny, too. He always made me laugh. I loved it when he came to see us. He would take us for a drive, or take us to get ice cream. Sometimes he would take us to his house, which I enjoyed. He had chickens, and we would go out and gather eggs if there were any. Once, he took us to a beautiful waterfall not far from his house. It was serene and peaceful. I walked along the creek and stood underneath the waterfall. It was a place of tranquility where a peaceful feeling filled one's mind. I know Charles helped Mother get through all of this. He really helped me, too. He always brightened our day, every time he came.

As time went by, I did slowly make progress in my recovery. I kept going to see Dr. Arisco. I kept taking my medication like I was supposed to. My energy level had slowed down now. I wasn't going fast and furiously anymore. I was sleeping now each night. My behavior was becoming more normal again. My mind was not racing as much anymore. My bizarre thoughts came less and less frequently. I was coming back to reality.

I had gotten the treatment I needed by going to Dr. Arisco and taking my medication properly. I did recover and move on with my life.

Starting Over Once Again

I was able to drive again. I was thinking clearly now. I needed to go back to work, so I went to a temporary agency and got jobs that would usually last for a few weeks. I finally got a permanent job where I thought I might stay for awhile. It was at a coffee company where they made their own coffee and sold it, and I got up and went to work with no problem, but I didn't talk much to my co-workers.

I found a place I thought I could afford to rent, just about ten miles from Mother's house. Mother helped with paying my expenses to move in. I was able to pay the rent on my own. It was a one-room building by a pool that was behind a house where the people I rented it from lived. There were no bedrooms, just one big open room. My bed was placed in one corner, and I had a small table and chairs in another corner. There was a built in desk at one end and I had a computer Mother had bought me sitting on it. The small kitchenette was outside, about twelve feet away from the building. The bathroom was also outside, adjoined to the kitchenette. It was fine for me, since I would be the only one living there. Tara, Kayla, and Trey would not be living with me; it saddened me that not even one of them was with me. I hadn't been able to see them once my mania had escalated. I was so happy now since I would be able to see them again. It had come to a point where it was best that Trey didn't come see me. Kayla left and went to her daddy's, and I wasn't able to be with her, either. I hadn't seen Tara since the last time she came to spend her spring break with me. I hadn't been able to take care of myself, much less take care of them, or provide for them. But now, they could be with me.

Tara and Kayla had moved back from Albuquerque. They were living back in Alba, Texas again with their grandparents. They would come to see me on weekends. All my children were coming to see me on weekends now that I had gotten better, and I was beside myself with joy when they were with me.

I only lived at the one room place for about two months. I thought I could afford to rent it, but it turned out I couldn't, so I moved back in with Debbie. I had had to rely on Mother, Debbie, and Teresa so heavily in my life. I thank God, they were always willing to help me; they never turned their back on me. I don't know where I would be if it was not for them. It is possible that I could have ended up living on the streets, or I could have even died. They're a family that anyone would love to have. I was so blessed God had given me such a wonderful mother and sisters.

I went from extreme energy to almost none again. Less than a year had gone by since I had gotten stable. I was taking my medication, but I just could not help feeling sad and down. Here I was, at thirty-seven years old, trying to start over again. I was trying to piece my life back together once again. I didn't have the desire to do much of anything. I was depressed again.

I met a girl, Rachel, while I was working at the coffee company who had come to work there shortly after me. We just hit it off, and we were able to talk easily with each other. We would go outside during our breaks and sit at a picnic table there. We would smoke, and she made me laugh as we talked. Being around her lifted my spirits. I was having good days and bad days.

Rachel told me she had a friend she wanted me to meet. She introduced me to him, and we starting seeing each other. Bob was a really nice man, but we really didn't have anything in common. Our conversations consisted of small talk, but I was glad to have a man in my life. A few months after we had been seeing each other, we were married and we moved into an apartment.

I had only worked at the coffee company about six months when I was told they didn't need me any longer. That was okay, because the only thing I really liked about the job was talking to Rachel. However, now I would be without a job again.

I lay in the bed almost every day since I wasn't working at the coffee company anymore. I couldn't bring myself to look for another job. I would get out of bed when it was almost time for Bob to come home from work, and I would fix supper for us. Afterwards, we would sit and watch TV for a little while. I often sat outside smoking. There was still very little conversation between us. I really didn't know why I married him. I just wanted to be married and have a good and happy relationship with someone, but marrying had not been the right thing to do. When it inevitably came to an end, and the marriage was annulled, I felt bad that I had married him because it had not been fair to him to be with a person who had not overcome depression. I didn't realize that if I didn't get out of the dark hole of depression, I would not be happy in any situation.

Now, I had no place to go, yet again. Teresa told me I could move in with her, and I took her up on her offer. Why couldn't I just get it together and get a place of my own? But the thought of that literally frightened me. Why couldn't I just look and find a job? I didn't see any way I could do that, either. I could hardly think of anything other than when the darkness and sadness would go away. When would I have a desire to find a job and get a place of my own? Why did I always seem to fall back into the darkness of depression?

Mother and I had not been talking as much lately. I was trying to live my life without relying on her so much. She had things going on in her own life as well that kept us from seeing each other as much.

Teresa went to work each morning. I just stayed in bed. I still found it hard to get up. I would lie there feeling nothing but sadness. There was no reason for me to get out of bed. I hated each and every day. I was tired all the time. I didn't want to do anything. I didn't even want to get out of the house. When would all this end? I wanted so desperately to find happiness again. Would it ever come my way again? I didn't go to see Dr. Arisco to discuss that I had become depressed again. I did contact him and let him know that I was feeling down, and he prescribed an anti-depressant for me. I had a reaction to it, however, and broke out in a rash. When I called his office to let him know about the rash, I was told to stop taking it. I had not been able to be completely open and honest with Dr. Arisco. I still did not realize how bi-polar had been affecting my life. I had been depressed so many times in my life I didn't know how important it was to discuss it with Dr. Arisco.

I laid around at Teresa's for a month or so. Her daughter, my niece Kelly, was working for a medical health system. Kelly told me I should apply there. I knew I had to get a job. I would never get better if I didn't get out of bed and do something.

I did apply at the medical health system and got a phone call a few days later asking me to come in for an interview. I was nervous going to the interview, but I made it through it just fine. I received a phone call a few days after the interview letting me know I had gotten the job. This really made me feel better. I had accomplished the first step in moving on with my life.

There was a lady who started to work there one month after I did. Her name was Jackie, and we would take our breaks together and talk. I was glad to have someone to talk to again, someone other than my family. I had withdrawn myself socially, but she made me feel like I could talk to her about myself. I told her all about my children, and she talked to me about her daughter. We got to be really close friends, and I definitely needed a friend now.

I was beginning to enjoy conversations with other people again. I was meeting a lot of friendly people at my new job. I actually liked going to work every day. Working almost always helped me to get past feeling so depressed.

A big part of my job duties now involved using a calculator. I knew ten-key by touch really well, but I had slowed down quite a lot now that I had gotten past my mania, and I became somewhat sluggish. I couldn't use the calculator as fast anymore, and I certainly wanted to do a good job. I had to focus on my speed in using the calculator in order to keep my job. I had told my boss about taking medication and that I was bi-polar. With her help, I was able to keep my job. I eventually was able to do my job well.

Debbie talked to me about getting an apartment. She had found some government apartments that she felt I could afford. She took me one day to see them. I wasn't excited about looking at them. I was leery and scared to live on my own. I didn't want to, but I had to move on with my life. I could not continue to rely on Debbie and Teresa. It was as if Debbie had to give me a push. Someone had to get me to wake up and realize I had to function on my own, and that's what Debbie did. She helped me out financially, paying a couple of my utility bills, and she told me I would be fine and that I would enjoy having my own place.

The apartment was one-bedroom. It was small, but it was plenty of room for me. Trey came every other weekend. He was smart, and he did well in school. When he was there, I wanted him to enjoy his time with me. Having Trey there made me happy. I missed him so very much. I wanted him to be with me all the time. I still felt guilt that I had told Vick he could live with him. There was no sense dwelling on it though. Trey was with me anyway, even though he wasn't at my home every day.

I worried all the time about how I would pay my bills. I had to pay my rent, car payment, my insurance, my child support, and groceries. I didn't ever buy many groceries. Because of all these expenses, I bought very little food. I usually just bought groceries for the weekends Trey would come. I just couldn't make myself believe that I could provide for myself. I was able to pay all of my bills every month, but that still didn't make me stop dwelling on my ability to pay them. This had been the first time I had lived on my own for any length of time since living in the apartment after Tara and Kayla's daddy and I had been divorced.

I was still somewhat depressed, but I was feeling better now, and I did want to get out and go places. After work I would go home, or sometimes I would go to Teresa's and eat supper with her and her family. Many days though, I would go to my apartment, go to bed, and stay there until the next morning. There just weren't many things to go do, and I didn't know anybody I could go somewhere with. Teresa called me every afternoon. She would try to encourage me that things would get better, and I tried hard to be positive about moving on with my life, but it was difficult.

I began to skip doses of my lithium. It didn't seem to be much different if I took it or if I didn't. I would take it one day, and then the next day, I wouldn't. I just hated taking medication. I hated the fact that I was bi-polar. I had, in some ways, come to terms with being bi-polar. I knew now since having had the severe episode with depression fifteen years ago and the severe manic episode ten years ago that I really had this disorder. After the last severe manic episode I had had about seven months ago, I began to realize that it could happen again. I still was not able to be as happy as I wanted to be. Now I was angry that I was bi-polar. Why was I bi-polar? Why did I have to be a person that had a mental illness?

I did start going places, and my moods were getting a little better. I was more positive, and I wasn't feeling as sad as I had been. I was still tired a lot of the time, though. I didn't seem to have many emotions anymore. Sometimes, I would want to cry, but the tears never came. Laughing was something I just couldn't do much at all. Since I had started taking lithium I had gained about thirty-five pounds. I didn't like the fact I wasn't the size I had been most of my life.

I was lonely. I wanted to meet a man again and have a relationship with someone. As before, I seemed to think I had to have a man in my life. I didn't want to be alone, but I was somewhat better about all of that. I had become content with living on my own now. I didn't go home and straight to bed much any more. I was getting a little more energetic.

I did meet a man at my apartment complex, and we talked in the evenings when I got home from work. We went out a few times. He talked about wanting to have a serious relationship, but I just wanted him to be my friend. This time, I didn't let myself slip into a relationship with someone I knew I wouldn't be happy with like I had done in the past. I realized I didn't have to be with the first man who took an interest in me.

I often wondered if I would ever find a man who would accept that I was bi-polar. I didn't want to have to tell that to a man again. I had already had to let go of a man that I had fallen in love with, and I had two failed marriages and an annulment. I needed to take time for myself.

I was talking to a lady I worked with one day. We started talking about where we had gone to school. She mentioned a guy named Tommy whom I had gone to elementary and junior high school with. She told me she still saw him sometimes, and I told her to tell him I said hi. She did see him after we talked about him, and did tell him I said hi.

She gave Tommy my phone number and he called me one night. I enjoyed talking to someone I had known in my past. We talked on the phone that night for a long time, and he told me he would like to see me, so I invited him to come over to my apartment one night.

He came to my apartment a couple of nights after we had talked on the phone. He knocked on the door. I was nervous, but excited to see him. I opened the door, and there he stood. He had on Wranglers and his cowboy hat and boots. I always was a sucker for cowboys. I didn't really know what to say to him. It didn't take long, though, and we found there were lots of things to talk about.

We sat on the couch and talked for hours that night. We reminisced about our school years, and it was actually very easy for me to talk to him. I hadn't been this comfortable talking to a man in a long while. We talked about people we had seen over the past years that we had gone to school with. He was funny and he made me laugh, which was something I needed. I had a great time with him and enjoyed the evening with him.

We talked on the phone almost every night now. He would came to my apartment often and we began to see a lot more of each other as time went on. Tommy eventually moved into my apartment with me. I fell in love with him, and I felt we could have a good relationship together.

About that same time, Kayla came back to live with me. She had just turned sixteen years old. I was excited for her to come back to live with me, but I worried about providing for her needs, just as I had done the last time she came to live with me. How would I be able to buy her nice clothes to wear to school? How would I be able to buy her all the things she needed? She would want a car now that she was sixteen, but I would not be able to afford to buy her one.

A couple of months after Tommy and Kayla came to live with me, we moved to a town about twelve miles from where we had been living. Trey was coming every other weekend, and at least one night during the week, just as he always had. He was growing up so fast. I wished that I could spend more time with him, and that summer I was able to because he came to stay with me until school started back. He was always a good boy, and he was kind-hearted. I knew that he would grow up to be a good man.

Tommy and I had been together for eight months now, and we decided to get married. We planned to just go to the justice of the peace. In the town we lived in now, we had friends that we both had gone to school with. They all got together and planned for us to have our wedding in our yard, so we wouldn't just go to the justice of the peace to get married. They decorated the yard in a country theme, with red, white and blue, and I appreciated what they did for us. A neighbor we knew that Tommy had known for a long while, and I had become friends with made our wedding cake. They had made our wedding so much more special to us. On the fourth of July, 2001, we were married.

Not Too Low, Not Too High

I continued taking my lithium on and off. I would still skip doses or go a few days or weeks without taking it. I would ration it until I went to get it filled again. I always thought that it would stay in my system long enough to keep me balanced. I didn't see that skipping doses would make a difference. When I did take my medication the way I was supposed to, I stayed stable. I just didn't seem to have as much energy as I wanted to have; I seemed to be sluggish and tired. I was like that even when I took it for several months at a time without skipping doses.

I would tell Debbie or Teresa every once in a while that I had not taken my medication in a few days. They would always say to me, "Melody, you can't do that. You have to take your medicine." Both of them would tell me if I needed the money to get the medicine just to let them know, and they would get it for me. When I would tell them I hadn't taken my medication, in some way it was as if I needed to hear them say to me I had to take it. Usually after they told me that, I would get my prescription filled and start taking it regularly again. I needed them to reinforce the fact that I must take my medication so that I would not end up sick again.

I should have realized that by telling my sisters I had not been taking my medication that it would make them worry. Why would I put them through the stress of that? It was not their responsibility to make sure I took my medication, it was mine. My sisters knew more than I did the importance of taking the lithium.

Taking medication seemed such a simple thing to do. For me, though, it was a reminder every day that I was bi-polar. I wanted to control my ups and downs all by myself.

I could tell when the depression and mania was getting out of control. I knew when I had better start taking my lithium every day again. I had come to know when I was getting too low or too high, and I thought I could handle it.

I used to think, after I had the first bout with depression, when I was pregnant with Kayla, that I had simply had a nervous breakdown. I didn't think that it would happen again. I had heard people talk about other people having nervous breakdowns when I was young. That's what had happened to me. It was just a nervous breakdown, and it would never happen again. That's what I chose to believe.

After four years of highs and lows that I didn't realize I was having, the fluctuations happened again, after the severe episode of depression, I ended up in a severe manic episode. Then, ten years passed, and another severe manic episode came again. In between those episodes, I had lows and highs for years. I couldn't deny it any longer.

Although I had gotten past the denial of being a person with bi-polar, I was still angry about it. I didn't understand why I had to be this way. Why was I considered and labeled as mental or even crazy? I was different from other people. Why couldn't I handle stress like other people could? Why did depression hover over me? Why couldn't I be happy? Why did mania take me out of reality? How did I get to be this way? I wanted it to just go away. I hated the fact that I had to take medication just to be normal.

When I hadn't taken my medication for a few weeks, I would notice little things that would worry me. I knew I could have another episode. I was always taking a big risk of a full blown episode happening from not taking my lithium daily. If I went more than a few days without the lithium, the signs of depression or mania came.

I would hear music sometimes when I went to bed, trying to go to sleep. I couldn't ever make out the words of the song, but I could tell someone was singing. I would get up out of my bed and look out my window. With Tommy lying beside me, I asked him one night if he heard music, and he told me he couldn't. I would try to figure out where the music was coming from. I never could figure it out. I would lie back down and try to get it out of my head. After doing this a few times, I would just try to ignore it. I would tell myself there was nobody playing any music, and nobody was singing. These were times when I wasn't sleeping well. Then I realized that each time I did this, I had gone without taking my medication for too long. I would then start taking it again.

Another sign was that when I was under a lot of stress, I would find myself wanting to stay in bed most of the time, or just the opposite, and wouldn't sleep good at night. I would feel like I had to do something to make the stress go away. If it didn't leave, I was going to be sick again. Each time I got really stressed out, I would start taking my medication again regularly in fear of having another severe episode.

One of the main things Dr. Arisco always told me was to watch my sleep patterns. If I went two or three nights without sleep, I knew I could be in trouble. Mania was usually coming on if I continued to go without sleep. I refused to take anything to help me sleep. I thought I didn't need that, either. All of this had to do with not wanting to take medication.

I stayed depressed a lot. I would go days where I didn't seem to have any energy at all. I went to work, but I didn't care about doing anything else except sitting at home. I felt almost unemotional. There were times I didn't cry when I thought I should be crying. There were times I really wanted to cry, but I just couldn't. When I got angry at something, I kept in bottled up and wouldn't talk about it. I hardly reacted to anything that was going on. I didn't get excited; most of the time I was emotionless, and I stayed depressed, except for the times when the energy of mania came every once and awile.

I didn't understand the whole concept of depression. When I was depressed, I really didn't consider it as depression. I thought depression was the way I was when I was pregnant with Kayla, and how I was after I had her. Real depression was when I found it hard to ever get up out of bed. It was when I thought I was a terrible person. It was when I thought nobody liked me. It was when I didn't feel like I could do anything right. It was when I didn't want to see anybody. It was when I didn't think about taking a bath. It was when I didn't care at all what I looked like. It was when I had bad thoughts that wouldn't go away. It was when I would wake up in cold sweats at night. It was when bad dreams came at night when I lay down to go to sleep. It was when I didn't think of eating anything. It was when I couldn't think of anything that was good. It was when I felt sad every minute of every day. It was when fears had overcome me. It was when I had no hope at all of getting out of the deep, dark hole I was in. Depression was when I wanted to die. This was why I did not think that I was depressed, when, truly, I was. If I didn't go to rock bottom, or think suicidal thoughts, I didn't believe I was depressed.

I would go to my appointments and tell Dr. Arisco about things that were stressing me out. I told him many times I didn't have any energy. There were times I would go to see him and I would cry during almost the whole session with him. I didn't cry very often, but during some of my visits with him, the tears flowed down my face. I did always feel better after seeing him. He knew the things I needed to hear to make me be aware that I did not want to have another full blown episode again.

Dr. Arisco would often ask if I wanted him to prescribe an anti-depressant for me. I always told him no. I would tell him I really wasn't depressed. I told him that because my whole concept of depression was all wrong. It probably would have helped for me to take an anti-depressant with my lithium. But, since my depression never descended to the point I had been depressed before, I didn't feel I needed it. There were times I thought it might be a good idea to try taking an anti-depressant, but when I thought about that, the next thought I would have is that I didn't need any more medication.

Depression had been such a recurring part of my life for so many years. I believed that the way I was was normal. It had come to be the way I lived my life. I didn't realize that I could actually live life without depression.

Dr. Arisco had a graph on an eight-by-ten sheet of paper. This graph had a straight line across the middle of it, and there were wavy lines above and below the straight line. He would show it to me time and time again. He would explain that the straight line was where I needed to be. If I didn't take my medication and continue my treatment, the chemicals in my brain could cause me to have the wavy lines. He would explain that the wavy lines showed the ups and downs I had with my bi-polar disorder. That graph made a big impact on me. It helped me to realize how the chemicals in my brain could get off-balance. It made me realize that the straight line is where I wanted to be.

At one point, I had stopped taking my medication for three months. I had lost about fifteen pounds and I liked the fact that I had lost the weight, and I knew it was because I had quit taking the lithium. I always knew the extra weight I had gained was from the lithium. When I would mention to Dr. Arisco about weighing more than I ever had since I had been taking lithium, he wouldn't really make a comment on it. Once, he did tell me that I could take other medications that could cause more weight gain than lithium. I didn't say anything to him again after that. I felt that he was telling me that a little weight was better than an episode. It was true; I did not want to be severely depressed or severely manic.

I couldn't go any longer without taking my lithium, though. There were too many signs that mania could be headed my way again. I had a lot more energy, and I talked a lot more than usual. I wasn't sleeping much at night. I really liked the way I was feeling, though. I loved having the energy, and I had the desire to keep it, but I knew it could eventually escalate to severe mania. I had gone too many nights without sleep. I realized it was possible that I could have another full blown episode of mania. I had to go see Dr. Arisco, so I made an appointment.

I told Dr. Arisco the day I went to my appointment that I had done a terrible thing. I told him I had stopped taking my lithium for three months. I had never gone more than a couple of weeks without taking it. He didn't seem to be surprised. He did tell me, like so many times before that I had to take my medication, and follow my treatment, which included keeping him informed of how I was doing. He always told me I did not want to get in the shape I had been in before. Again, he told me I did not want my sisters to go through what they had gone through when I had my last manic episode. He really made me think about what my sisters had gone through. He made me realize how very difficult it was for them to watch me go through it. I had frightened my sisters. After all, they had been told then that I could die. Dr. Arisco reminded me of that, also. I thought for a long time that I was the only one that suffered, but now, after the many times Dr. Arisco told me how horrible it was for my sisters to go through it, I realized they suffered significantly as well.

I think Tommy, my husband, thought that it was normal for me to be the way I was. The majority of the time we had been together, I stayed in a depressed state. Like me, he didn't realize I could be any different. We would talk sometimes about my being bi-polar. I would tell him about things I did during my episodes and the shape I was in during those times. When I did get really stressed, I would always tell him. "I can't take much more of this." I would tell him I could get sick again. He knew when I told him I could get sick that I was talking about having another episode. He always tried to understand, although I know he really couldn't completely. Tara, Kayla, Trey, and my sisters always thought I was doing really well. I had become a person with bi-polar who kept myself from going too low or too high. I had learned how long I could go without taking my medication. I always knew when I had to start taking it the right way. It was very risky for me to try to control my ups and downs myself. My family, of course, didn't know I did this. As long as I didn't get too low or too high, they considered me as doing well. I thank God I didn't get in the state of mind I had been in before.

I went to my appointments to see Dr. Arisco every three months. The appointments were supposed to decrease from every three months to every six months. I would ask him about being able to lower my dosage of my lithium, he would tell me we would talk about that my next visit. My goal was to be able to go six months before having to go see him again. There always seemed to be something that made me need and want to go see him before the six months came. My dosage of lithium was never changed. That next visit, I would be in a state that showed Arisco that it wouldn't be good to lower the dosage.

I don't know if Dr. Arisco knew I had not always taken my lithium the way he prescribed it to me; I didn't tell him. I eventually felt that he did, though. He had always made it very clear to me that if I wasn't willing to respond to treatment and take my medication that he couldn't help me. That was so true.

I had to take responsibility and take care of myself. I learned that the hard way. I feel sure I could have prevented some of the downs of depression and the highs of mania if I would have just taken my medication the way I was supposed to. I was hurting my family by being dishonest with them about taking my medication correctly. I had realized that it was not only me that suffered with bi-polar; my family suffered through it with me. As Dr. Arisco had told me all through the years of seeing him, "You don't want your sisters to go through all that again."

He finally made me realize that they were the ones who were supporting me and had always supported me throughout my life. They were the ones who put so much of their lives aside to take care of me when I was sick with an episode of mania or depression. It took me way too many years to realize that I must do what was necessary to control my illness as much as I possibly could. I had never taken my mental illness seriously enough. If it had not been for my family, I don't know if I would be dead or alive today.

And, if it hadn't been for going to my appointments with Dr. Arisco and listening to the things he told me, I feel that I would have ended up in another severe episode. He was the one who over the years made me understand how my illness affected my life. After seeing him for five years, I began to realize I was hindering myself from having a life without the continuance of highs and lows.

For several years, I believed that I could control my ups and downs on my own. But, in fact, if I had taken my medication the way I was supposed to, it would have been possible to have prevented the roller coaster of the highs and lows that had plagued me for so many years.

CHANGES IN ME

It is very important that I have lab work done from time to time when taking lithium, because I need the lithium level to be checked. Also, I need to check for kidney and liver damage, as well as having a blood test to check my thyroid. I do have thyroid disease. It's necessary for me to take medication for it, also. Another thing that is necessary for me to have is a urinalysis.

When the time came around to have lab work done, I was told I needed to have a twenty-four hour urinalysis test. The lab results were sent to Dr. Arisco. When I went to my next appointment with Dr. Arisco he mention lithium concentration. He told me that this could be the beginning of possible kidney damage. I didn't understand exactly what he was telling me. My urine had been virtually colorless for awhile. I didn't know if this was something to do with that.

When Dr. Arisco told me that this could be the beginning of possible kidney damage, it scared me. He had told me times before that lithium could cause kidney failure. I did not want to take lithium any longer. I couldn't face kidney failure on top of everything else.

I looked at Dr. Arisco and said, "I want to stop taking lithium."

He had told me more than once that we would need to consider another medication to control my bi-polar disorder after seven to ten years. It could cause problems after taking it for a certain length of time. It could become less effective. I had been taken lithium for seven years now.

When I told him I wanted to stop taking the lithium, he began telling me about a drug that was fairly new for treating bi-polar disorder, a drug that also treated epilepsy. It was scary to stop taking the lithium after so many years. I knew that it could be difficult to find the right medication for each individual person. I trusted Dr. Arisco's judgment, as I always had. I knew that he would recommend a medication that he felt I might respond to, and would help control my ups and downs.

I began taking the new medication, Lamictal, which he prescribed to me. He gave me samples, and I was to work my way up to the dosage I needed. Once I got up to that dosage, I only had to take one pill a day. I loved that since I had never wanted to take a lot of pills, as I had done when I was in University Park Hospital. I had hated that I had had to take four pills of lithium a day in addition to my thyroid medication.

I saw a huge change in myself in the first few weeks. I lost about twenty-five pounds in about four to six weeks, but I didn't understand why I was losing so much weight so fast. I was the size I had been almost all my life now, except when I had taken lithium. I was glad of that, but I was concerned about it. I didn't know if it was normal to lose the weight so fast, especially since I had been the same size for seven years now. My weight had normally been around one hundred forty-five pounds for these seven years.

I also had so much more energy, and I loved that. I was almost always in a good mood. I was talking more to my kids. I was more interested in the things going on in their lives. I would get excited about things. I felt good about myself. I was enjoying conversations with people more. I was being more opinionated. I felt like I was coming out of a shell that I had been living in for a long, long time. I wanted to get out of the house and go places and do things now. I was keeping my house clean every day. I felt really happy. It had been many, many years since I had felt this good. I couldn't believe that the Lamictal was helping me this quickly. I hadn't anticipated any extreme difference by switching medicines until a couple of months or more of taking it. Actually, I never dreamed I could feel this way at all.

I was concerned about all of this, though, so I made an appointment to see Dr. Arisco to ask him if these things should be happening to me. I needed to hear what he thought, and if it was normal.

I went to my appointment and I told him about all the changes with me since I had started taking the Lamictal. I wanted to know if I had too much energy, or if the weight loss was something I should be concerned about. I felt like I might be getting manic again. The way I was feeling seemed too good to be true.

He told me the lithium had kept a lot of fluid in me, and that's why I had lost all the weight. He told me the energy was normal, too. He assured me that I was all right. He told me that Lamictal was working well for me. It was working very well for me, and I was so glad it was.

Christmas time was just around the corner. Tommy and I had been short on money. I was stressed and worried because I didn't know how we would be able to buy gifts for my kids, or Tommy's daughter, Amber, and her two sons, Price and Carter, and for his son T.C. I didn't know how I would be able to give my family a good Christmas. I felt horrible. This was going to be the worst Christmas ever. I know Christmas is definitely not about all the presents, but I wanted our children to have a present from Tommy and me for Christmas.

Tommy had not been working for a few months, and it was putting a strain on us financially. I was trying to keep up with all the bills with what I was bringing home, and it wasn't enough.

I had three nights when I hadn't been able to sleep. My mind was racing again when I went bed, and I could not shut it off. I was worrying day after day about how we were going to make ends meet. I knew I had to get some sleep and get the racing thoughts to stop.

I always watched my sleeping patterns. If more than two or three nights pass without my getting good sleep, I get concerned about it. Going without sleep is a sign I always watch for. It's often the beginning of mania with me.

I had become the person I knew when I was in my late teens and early twenties, and that was the time I remember that I felt true happiness. I felt good then and I felt good about myself. I enjoyed life. The change in me was making me realize that I was so much like the person I was before I ever knew of depression or mania. I knew now depression and mania had been my company all through these years.

One night I was tossing and turning in bed. I had gone without much sleep for three or four nights now. I had to talk to somebody, and Debbie had always been the one I would talk to when I felt I might be slipping into another episode. She understood it all more than anyone else I knew. Debbie had battled with her own depression at one point in her life. She also has obsessive compulsive disorder. Debbie could relate to some of the things I had dealt with being bi-polar. She could usually clue in on the signs of it in me.

I got up that night and called Debbie.

When she answered the phone I asked her, "What are you doing?" I was trying to hold my tears back, but I couldn't. I just started crying.

"What's wrong, Melody? What is it?"

"I haven't been able to sleep for a few nights. I'm scared. I don't know if I'm getting sick, if I'm becoming manic, or what." Debbie, too, knew that going without sleep was the first sign to watch for. She could sense that I was very upset.

"Do you want me to come over?"

"No; I don't know." I didn't want to bother her, nor did I want her to think that I might be slipping into another episode.

I knew she would be concerned. There were no guarantees that I couldn't have another episode of either manic or depression.

With calmness but concern, Debbie said, "I will come over if you want me to."

"It's late; I know you need to go to bed," I replied

"It's alright, Melody. I will come right now."

Debbie always made it clear to me that if I needed her she would be there for me, just as Teresa always had. They had always told me to let them know if I felt I was getting sick. My sisters have always, no matter what, done whatever they could to help me in any situation I was in.

I was crying and couldn't stop. I needed to have her come so I could talk to her about everything I was feeling.

"Yes, I want you to come," I said.

"I'm on my way, I'll be there in just a few minutes," she answered.

Tommy was in the bed, and he asked me what was wrong. I explained to him that I had been worried and had not been sleeping. I told him I had called Debbie, and she was coming over so I could talk to her. He stayed in the bed, knowing why I had called Debbie to come. He had tried to assure me everything would be fine, but I needed more than to hear him say that. I needed Debbie to talk to.

I paced the floors while I was waiting for Debbie to come. I tried to sit still, but I couldn't. I was anxious, and didn't know for sure what was happening with me. I hadn't been sad. I felt really good until it got closer to Christmas. I had just started dwelling on how we were not going to be able to give mine and Tommy's children and grandchildren anything for Christmas, or even a nice Christmas dinner. Tommy and I both had been stressed about our money situation. We had been struggling to pay our bills, keep our electricity on, the rent, and our car payments. I didn't know how we were going to get ourselves back to where we could pay our bills.

When Debbie got there, I felt relief wash over me. I felt that everything would be all right. We sat down at my kitchen table. I began to tell her I hadn't been sleeping for the past few nights. I told her I didn't know why, and that it was worrying me.

I said to her with hope, "I just can't be getting sick. I don't want that to happen again."

I explained to her that money had been so tight for quite a while, and I didn't see any way it was going to get better. I was trying to pay our bills since Tommy had not been working. There was just not enough money to go around. Our bills kept getting farther behind, and I was sure we could possibly lose our vehicles and have to move out of the house we were renting.

With tears in my eyes, I said to Debbie, "We're going to have a horrible Christmas. I'm not going to be able to get my kids anything."

Christmas had never been filled with lots and lots of gifts in our house. I was always satisfied to be able to get my kids just a few things. They never expected a lot for Christmas, and they were always thankful for what they got. All three of them always made it clear to me that it didn't matter if they didn't get expensive things. They were appreciative for what they did get.

I said to Debbie, "I know that Jesus' birth is what Christmas is all about. I know Tara, Kayla and Trey would understand if I weren't able to get them a lot for Christmas."

I felt bad for telling Debbie all these things, because I knew it broke her heart to see me sad and stressed out with all that was going on with me. She sat there at the kitchen table with me and listened to me talk about everything that was stressing me out. Debbie always listened to all I wanted and needed to say. When she saw that I had said most of what was on my mind, she began her reassurance that this would all work out. I talked to her about how really well the Lamictal was working for me. She knew that it had made a drastic change in me for the better.

I ask her if maybe I was getting too high, and if maybe I could be getting manic. There had been so many changes in me, and I was almost overwhelmed that I could really feel happy and have energy and want to do things, instead of just sitting at the house most of the time. My life had become so much more enjoyable. What was happening to me now?

Then she told me she wanted to give me some money so I would have a nice Christmas. I did not want her to do that.

"Debbie, I don't want you to give me money; I don't want anybody to help me," I said.

She had tears in her eyes, too, and she looked at me with such desire to take all my stress away. She said, "I can't have a good Christmas."

I didn't understand why she had told me she couldn't have a good Christmas.

Puzzled, I asked her, "What do you mean? Why can't you have a good Christmas?"

The tears were really streaming down her face now, as they were mine. We talked about different things that we had gone through in our lives that were hard for us to get through.

She said to me, "Melody, I can't have a good Christmas if you don't."

I could see in her eyes she meant every word of that. As always, she never wanted me to struggle, or have sadness in my life. Being very close sisters, we took on each other's pain and heartaches, and we wanted to make all the problems go away.

Debbie and I talked and cried together for a few hours. She told me that because of everything that was happening with me, it was normal that I would have trouble sleeping, since I was worrying about how I was going to take care of everything. She told me I was doing so well.

She said to me with total belief in her eyes, "I just feel sure that you are not getting sick. You are not getting manic."

All of the emotions were something I had not felt in a long while. I didn't realize the way I was feeling was a normal part of dealing with stress. It frightened me. I was facing things more in a normal way now. I used to just crawl in bed and want to bury my head so I wouldn't have to face things that I needed to deal with, and it would just make me sink into depression.

Then she told me we were going to make an appointment with Dr. Arisco the next morning. I agreed to that. Before Debbie left, we had stopped talking about what I had been dwelling on. She had made me realize that my fear of getting sick was not warranted. We were even laughing about other things before she left my house. She had completely calmed me down.

I crawled up in the bed after she left, and I actually went to sleep. I had desperately needed to spill out all that I was feeling and holding inside.

I made an appointment the next day to see Dr. Arisco. Debbie went with me, and soon after we got to Dr. Arisco's office, he came out to the waiting room and called me back. Debbie and I went into the room where I always spoke with him.

As always, he asked, "How is everything?"

I said right off, "Well, I can't sleep."

I told him all the things that I had told Debbie. I explained to him about all the stress I'd been having. I went on to tell him that I was afraid that I might be getting manic again.

I had last gone to see him after taking Lamictal for just a few months, out of concern because I had lost about twenty-five pounds very quickly and I had so much more energy than I had had in a very long time. I had thought my energy level might be getting too high. Now, I was concerned because I was so stressed out and couldn't sleep.

Dr. Arisco told me that under the circumstances, anyone would be stressed. It was normal. We talked about all of it for a few minutes, and he asked Debbie what she thought. He always asked Debbie and Teresa what they thought about different circumstances I was going through if they went to see him with me. Debbie made her comments to him, telling him that she saw that I was doing very well on the Lamictal. She told him that she felt all the stress I had been having was why I felt the way I did.

He prescribed sleeping pills for the nights I couldn't sleep. Once again, after going to my visit with Dr. Arisco, I could rest assured that I was not getting sick. The stress I had been having lessened. My sleepless nights became fewer and fewer, and I didn't need the sleeping pills any longer. I knew, though, if I went for three or more nights of sleep, I needed something to help me sleep until my sleeping patterns got back on track.

Teresa is whom I find strength from. She and I have a very close relationship, also. We talk about different things than what Debbie and I talk about sometimes. Teresa always tells me I am strong, and that I'll make it through what ever comes my way. She tells me there's a purpose for all things that happen in our lives. When I need her, she's there. She tells me to pray, and have faith. I always tell her I pray God will guide me through my days, and that I always keep my faith. I love my sisters dearly, and they love me just the same. My sisters and I completely have faith in God, which gives us hope, and this is the reason we make it through our trials and tribulations.

Tommy and I continued to struggle financially. It was causing a strain on our marriage. Tommy had been adjusting to the changes with me since I had begun to take the new medication, just as all my family had. I had told Tommy through the years of our marriage that stress was a big reason why I had had the episodes I did in the past. He always tried to understand, yet it was difficult because he had never seen me in a severe episode. Throughout most of out marriage Tommy had seen me be a person who wasn't very energetic; one who retired to my bed and slept a lot. For the most part, I had been depressed much of our entire marriage. He was realizing that now.

The financial problems and other problems that we were dealing with had to be taken care of for us to have a happy, healthy marriage. My being so different had been an adjustment for him as well as for me since I had started taking Lamictal. He had not ever seen the side of me that I had now become. It was a good thing; however, voicing my feelings and talking more about our struggles with him was something I had not done a lot with Tommy until now.

I had gotten to the point that I decided we needed time apart and put forth the effort to get our marriage back to where it needed to be. I knew I couldn't go on with the stress I was under. He agreed, but it was difficult to do. We were in love, and we had grown to become each other's best friend. Neither one of us wanted our marriage to come to an end.

When Tommy and I separated, I refused to go back to live with Debbie or Teresa as I had many times. I was much stronger now, and I was much more confident that I could get a place, and be on my own, and take care of finances myself. I made up my mind that I would do what was necessary for me and not rely on Debbie or Teresa to help me. I felt capable now to take responsibility for myself.

I applied at the department store where Debbie worked and was hired. It was part-time which would be sufficient with working at my other job, and I would make enough money to be able to pay my living expenses. I saved my money so I would be able to pay the deposit it took to move into the apartment I had found. I was determined to do this. I did stay with Debbie, but only for two weeks, and then I had enough money to pay the deposit. I did what I knew I could do to make it on my own. It was an accomplishment to be able to work two jobs and take care of myself financially. I would not have been able to do that just a couple of years back because I did not believe I could.

Tara was twenty-three years old now, Kayla was twenty-one, and Trey was fourteen. Trey had begun to stay at my home much more for the past five years.

Tommy and I struggled with getting our marriage back where it needed to be again. It had been nine months now since we had been separated. There were things we both realized that needed to change in our relationship.

After close to a year, we wanted to be together again. We knew we didn't want to be apart. We were determined to do what was necessary to make our marriage a happy one. Neither he nor I wanted our marriage to fail. We live in Chandler, Texas, and enjoy our life together.

My Mother was diagnosed with Alzheimer's disease in 2001. I never did thank her for all she had done for me, or sit down and talk to Mother and ask her how she had felt seeing her daughter live with depression and mania, and how she made it through it. Years ago when I became severely depressed, she did not want to accept that I needed help to get through it. When she finally did, she was willing to do all she could to make everything all right. She was the strongest person I had ever known, and I will always admire her for being the person she was. I have the most wonderful Mother, and I will always be thankful to God for her. I think Mother and Daddy would be proud of me now. I would love for them both to see what life has brought me.

I knew to always be thankful. I had learned that from Momma Phillips, my Daddy's mother. I heard her say so many times she was thankful for all she had. I knew when I went to her house there would be candy to eat, because she always had a pretty candy dish full with candy that sat on her coffee table in the living room. She lived in Lindale, Texas, close to downtown. She didn't drive so she walked where she needed to go, if it was to the post office, or to church, and other places that were close by. She had a sense of humor, and a sharp mind. She raised her two sons, and four daughters on her own as her husband had died when my daddy was a very young boy. She was a very gracious woman who loved her family greatly. She was ninety-six when she passed away in 2006. She had told her family many times she was ready to go home. And now, she's in Heaven with her son, my Daddy. I loved her dearly, and she will always have a very special place in my heart.

MELODY'S BACK

The love and support from my family and friends, and all of their prayers, is what helped me survive my illness all through the nineteen years since I was diagnosed with bi-polar. What also helped was having an exceptionally good doctor who has brought me to a better understanding of bi-polar disorder and how it affects me.

Many times through my episodes, it was my children who gave me a strong will to live. My children and I have a very close relationship now. We always did, but now it's so much better. My children finally see their momma being a happy person.

Tara continues her desire to learn all she can. She graduated with a bachelor's degree in Psychology with honors in 2003. Tara says, "I feel like I met my mom for the first time."

Kayla had a desire to be a momma herself. She was blessed with a beautiful baby girl in 2006, whom she named Jadeyn Hope. Kayla says, "Now you will enjoy doing things with Jadeyn and will be a great Grandma to her."

Trey is a sophomore in high school, now, and he was a member of the local volunteer fire department. He enjoys playing football in school. When there's something brought up about the manic episode I had when he was six, he says, "That's when you were crazy."

Now my children understand why I was the way I was for so much of their lives. They are pleased to see who I am today.

Debbie and Teresa say, "We have gotten our sister back."

Tommy and I have a good marriage now. He says "You're happy, you have more energy, you're more outgoing, and you care about things more, and it makes me happy to see you enjoy life."

They all watch for my signs of depression and mania. There have been times when they've talked amongst themselves asking each other if they think that I'm all right. They've asked me several times if I'm taking my medication. I used to get angry with them for asking me that, but now I realize they ask me because they love me, and they don't want to see me slip into another episode.

Once, Kayla was at my house and she found an empty bottle of my medication on my dresser. She brought it to me and asked, "What's this?"

I told her to go look in the medicine cabinet in my bathroom. There, she found that I had a full bottle of my medication. She came out from the bathroom and said, "All right then."

I take responsibility for taking care of myself and do what is necessary so that I can possibly prevent another episode to occur. There are no guarantees that I won't. But if I'm tuned into to my illness, it's less likely that I will. I take my medication always and go to see Dr. Arisco on a regular basis. I watch for the signs of depression or mania coming my way so that they won't take over me and swing out of control. When stress comes my way, I make sure it doesn't consume me. I do this not only for myself, but for my family, also.

I now can go longer than three months for an appointment with Dr. Arisco. He has told me several times that I'm just as normal as the next person. After hearing this from him through the years, he has made me realize I am a normal person. Even though I am bi-polar, I am not crazy.

I began to educate myself about my illness for the past three years, much more so than I ever had. I thought for a long time that since I was bi-polar, I knew all the effects and all there was to know about it. I have found that I didn't know nearly all there is to know about bi-polar disorder. I am bi-polar, level I, and each level is different from the other. Each person has his or her own signs and symptoms. It has helped me tremendously to read about it and listen to other people talk about it. I was ignorant of the whole concept of bi-polar disorder, just as many people are. Even I cannot completely understand it all. After all, it affects the most complicated part of the body, the brain.

Mental illness desperately needs to be brought up to the table and taken seriously. Society needs to know the severity of it and have more understanding of bi-polar disorder and mental illness in general. It affects so many adults, and it also affects so many of our children. It's a life threatening illness. In the depths of depression, it can cause people to commit suicide. In the highs of mania, it can cause people to harm themselves or others.

Individuals with bi-polar disorder and other mental illnesses do not want to be pushed aside. We want society to accept us, without any of the stigmatism and discrimination.

In August 2007, I organized the East Texas Bi-Polar support group; There is Hope! We give each other support in coping and providing information. Giving encouragement and hope, and to bring more understanding and awareness. I enjoy the meetings, and I benefit significantly from them.

My next goal in my life is to form a Bi-polar Awareness Foundation since I am a person that lives with bi-polar. It would be a foundation that would provide information for individuals that live with any mental illness, their family and friends, and society. It would make it possible for our support group to do more to bring awareness to bi-polar. My hopes are that the foundation would grow to be able to help people that can not afford the expenses for their treatment and the medications they need. I want to provide names of facilities, doctors, and other resources where treatment is available because so many people do not know where to turn for help. Also, I want to raise funds to go towards more research, which is much needed. Mental illness needs to be recognized as a serious illness as other ones are. This is my passion, and my mission. It's a dream that I would love to see come true.

I was buried under my illness for so many years, and I have come so far from where I was. I have a functional, fulfilling, and happy life. I am back to the person I truly am, and it's a great feeling.

I thank God for His ultimate love and guidance, which has brought me to where I am today. I believe God took me through a difficult journey and gave me a testimony to share, and He has given me the ability to write my story. My hope and prayer is that I will bring awareness and some understanding of how this illness can affect people's lives.

I also hope and pray that someone will read my book and know that they are not alone, and to know there is hope!

Hi, my name is Melody, I have bi-polar disorder.

The Journey Of Life

The journey of life brings us at times much joy
Other times it brings us much suffering
Also there is heartache, but God mends our heart
We can always rest assure God will guide us through the journey of life

God has given us family, friends, and even strangers
That can celebrate with us, and comfort us through difficult times
He also gives them to us so we can share our joys with each other
God wants us to know we are never alone, even when we think we are

If we will keep our faith in God, we will know all will be taken care of
We seem to forget the times of joy and happiness we've had
When times turn to the pain and suffering
Even then, God is still carrying us through the journey of life

If we share our blessings and testimony we have
We are helping others through the journey of life
We need to share our joys so others can celebrate with us
We need to realize, it's a blessing to have them

We cannot understand why we go through turmoil,
We need to remember God has a plan for the journey of life
Even when we don't think He is with us, He truly is
The journey of life is difficult, we will make it through it, with God

Melody Hope